SEVENTEEN
Guardian Angels

CYNTHIA PAPIERNIAK

Copyright © 2013 Cynthia Papierniak

All rights reserved.

ISBN: 1482338149

ISBN 13: 9781482338140

Library of Congress Control Number: 2013902625

CreateSpace Independent Publishing Platform North Charleston, SC

For Anna
You have given me so much more
than I could ever give you

Overture

A therapist once told me, "Don't kid yourself. If you enter a room with one hundred people, there is a good chance that thirty to forty of them have experienced some degree of child abuse. Unfortunately, the human species can be cruel to their young."

I am in that thirty to forty percent. I experienced sporadic physical abuse, constant verbal abuse, and certain emotional abuse from my mother. I also encountered people along the way who kept me on life's path. Some saved me from my mother, some saved me from myself, and some offered their friendship, compassion, or guidance. These were my guardian angels.

When I think about guardian angels, the first image that comes to mind is Clarence from the movie *It's a Wonderful Life*. He was the angel that jumped from a bridge into the frigid river so George Bailey would dive in and save him. Clarence jumped in the river knowing beforehand that George was contemplating ending his life. I have also read stories of people miraculously showing up and assisting someone, but later there is no trace of that individual. This leads one to believe that whoever provided help in that desperate moment might have been a celestial being.

My guardian angels walked and worked on planet Earth. They include a teacher, Girl Scout leader, neighbor, librarian, football coach, college roommate, psychologist, psychiatrist, nurse, aunt, minister, piano teacher, and friends. Some of my guardian angels offered me their attention and kindness. Some actively intervened and made sure I got help, and a few were professionals that I chose to help me, their selection being a bit of a gamble. Others extended their hand in friendship, offered me a different perspective of myself, or guided my spirit. There were those that listened when I cried, and others that made me laugh at myself.

Sadly, some of my guardian angels (those whose full names are given) are now shining their halos and will never read these words. To avoid public embarrassment, I have abbreviated names of the guardian angels that are alive and still helping others. This story has been created from my memory, and although the sentiment remains true, some of the details may be altered.

This book is a paean to seventeen of those guardian angels. When I reflect on how my life was changed by these people, I would like to think that their caring was not a coincidence but a meaningful encounter. To all my guardian angels, I offer my deepest respect, sincere gratitude, and enduring love.

Table of Contents

First Guardian Angel   1
Sue DeMoulin

Second Guardian Angel   5
Dorothy L. McLaren

Third Guardian Angel   11
Jopi Bannink

Fourth Guardian Angel   15
Judith G.

Fifth Guardian Angel   27
Stephen T.

Sixth Guardian Angel   31
Dr. Gerald Edwards

Seventh Guardian Angel   35
Dr. Herbert J. Hauer, Ph.D.

Eighth Guardian Angel   47
Rowena Staniseski Rotolo

Ninth Guardian Angel   51
Diane T.

Interlude I	55
Tenth Guardian Angel Lt. Serena Y.	63
Interlude II	67
Eleventh Guardian Angel Dr. S., M.D.	73
Twelfth Guardian Angel Kathy R. W.	99
Thirteenth Guardian Angel Kathleen Jackson, R.N.	101
Fourteenth Guardian Angel Victoria Grigas-Hoffman	105
Fifteenth Guardian Angel Dr. E., M.D.	109
Sixteenth Guardian Angel Dr. Mike F.	117
Seventeenth Guardian Angel Rev. Erik Gustafson	119
Conclusion	121
Coda	133
Encore	135
Bravo! Brava!	137

"Scars speak louder than the sword that caused them."
-----Paulo Coelho
Manuscript Found in Accra

Lillian Kanapicki, LCDR Kasimir Kanapicki, USN
Cynthia, Age 9 Charles, Age 5

Chicago, Illinois (1956)

Mrs. Sue DeMoulin

Navy wife, Girl Scout leader, Coronado, California (1956-1961)

1956. Ten years old. I will remember Mrs. DeMoulin as the first person that I reached out to as a child. As very young children my mother was strict with both my brother and me, but neither of us knew any better—so we marched to her cadence. As I got older, things started to change.

Mrs. DeMoulin was a Navy wife whom my mother had met previously in Japan, and now both her husband and my dad were stationed at the Naval Air Station North Island in Coronado, California. Mrs. DeMoulin had four girls. Sharon, the oldest, and I were both in fifth grade. The DeMoulins lived in a rambling house a few blocks from the school. I lived about five blocks from the school. Frequently I was invited to their home after school, and I had fun. Things were loose; there were toys and games in the living room and books on the floor.

In contrast, my house was like a museum. It would drive my mother crazy if the books on the shelves weren't arranged in descending-height order. No toys were allowed in the living room. Music must be returned to the piano bench. We were not allowed to eat away from the dining room. Clothes were hung up on hangers that were each labeled for the specific garment. For example, the navy blue sweater needed to be hung on the hanger that said "navy blue sweater." Do you remember playing the game

Monopoly? After you finished the game, you stashed the money and the railroad cards under the playing board and put the box away. Well, we did the same, but the next time we opened the box, the money would be grouped according to denomination. My mother organized play money.

Once, when I came home from a sleepover at the DeMoulin's, I said, "Mommy, I had so much fun at Sharon's."

"What did you call me?"

"Mommy." I had heard Mrs. DeMoulin's daughters call their mother "mommy" and was imitating them.

"I am your mother, and you will call me by that name."

"Yes, mother."

If there was a defining moment that established the tonality of our future relationship, I believe that statement was a striking chord. However, at that time I was just a little surprised, and I did not dwell on what she said.

Mrs. DeMoulin asked me if I wanted to join her Girl Scout troop, and I leaped at the suggestion. I participated actively, and the troop elected me secretary. I wrote my first minutes carefully. In sterling penmanship, I wrote who was at the meeting, how much money was in the bank, what the program was, what our charity project was, and who brought the refreshments. I asked my mother to review what I had written, because I wanted it to be done well.

Well, she took a look at what I had written, and she said that it was hardly what could be called proper minutes. She went and found her Robert's Rules of Order and found some minutes she had taken for some group. She made me rewrite my minutes using her template. When I finished it looked like a congressional record. I knew how to type, and she then told me it should be typed.

When I went to the next meeting, I read my revised minutes and everybody was so impressed. But it was hard work. I used her template a few more times, but then I just got tired of doing it. Finally, I didn't do it at all. My mother asked me if I had written the minutes for the next meeting and I told her I had (I lied), but thankfully she didn't ask to see them.

I went to the next meeting without the minutes. I was so embarrassed not to have the minutes ready that I couldn't enter the front door with all the scouts. Instead, I just waited in Mrs. DeMoulin's backyard not knowing what to do. I finally mustered the courage to knock on her back door. I told her that I was so sorry, that I didn't have the minutes, and because of that I couldn't come to the meeting.

She said, "Oh, Cynthia, that's not important, please come in. It will be all right." I started to cry, "Please don't tell my mother I didn't do the minutes. She will be so angry." She said, "It's OK. Go upstairs and wash your face and come to the meeting." When I entered the room, Mrs. DeMoulin announced that the minutes of the last meeting would be read at the next meeting. (Simple.) I recorded the minutes of Girl Scout Troop 150 only one more time. At the next meeting Mrs. DeMoulin said, "Girls, Cynthia has done this very well, but I think someone else can take over." (Grace extended.)

The DeMoulin's house was closer to the school than ours, and it was always inviting to walk to Sharon's house after school. But there were strict rules at my home. I was not allowed to go to anyone's house unless I asked for permission before school, or I had to call my mother within fifteen minutes of school dismissal if I went to someone else's home. Sharon asked me over, and I went to her house, but I couldn't reach my mother. The phone was busy; I tried again—still busy. My fifteen minutes was almost up. I told her I had to leave and go home.

But I also had to go to the bathroom. As a fifth grader, I nervously weighed my options. I could go to the bathroom at Sharon's and be late or run home and almost be on time. I started to run home; I was worried and anxious, and the urine just came out of me. I knew that if I went home my mother would be angry not only that I hadn't returned in the allotted time, but that I had also peed in my pants. Instead I turned around and walked back to Mrs. DeMoulin's.

She looked at my wet shoes and instantly knew what had happened. She was so kind. I told her that my mother was going to be furious because I hadn't called her, and this is what Mrs. DeMoulin did for me. She called up my mother and told her that the reason I hadn't called was because she was on the phone with her husband. Also, since Sue's husband had asked her to pick him up from the base, she said that she would drop me off on the way. Therefore I had time to clean up.

Mrs. DeMoulin rescued me one more time about four years later. The DeMoulins were living in Laurel, Maryland, and we were temporarily at Patuxent River, Maryland. My mother called Mrs. DeMoulin shortly after arriving in Patuxent, and of course told her that I, her straight-A daughter, had done a lot of stupid things during the move. She went on to say that the temporary quarters were not air-conditioned, it was hot as hell, and she had just about had it with me.

Sue called back the next day, invited me out to Laurel to spend the weekend with Sharon and her sisters, and said she would pick me up. I had a wonderful time. Mrs. DeMoulin took us to a movie, *The Parent Trap*, took us for a haircut, and then to lunch. She told me that I had blossomed into being a lovely young lady. She even told me that I looked a little like Hayley Mills, the star of *Parent Trap* (whom I adored). It wasn't quite true, but it made me feel pretty special.

When my parents picked me up from the weekend, Dad and my brother Charles went inside their house, and Mother and I remained in the car. I told my mother that I really had fun, and I thanked her for letting me come. Mrs. DeMoulin came out to the car briefly to wish us goodbye, and she told Mother what a pleasure it was to have me visit. All my mother could say afterwards was, "You know, when people sew their own clothes, they always look homemade."

My mother was keen on reciprocity. If someone did something nice for her she always had to reciprocate. And we all heard about the times that she just "had to reciprocate" even if she didn't like the person or felt that she had been unwillingly or unwittingly obligated. I learned to hate that word. However, this time reciprocity meant that my parents invited Sharon and one of her sisters to come with our family to the Smithsonian Institution. I had two pleasant weekends while in Patuxent River.

Mrs. DeMoulin did one more thing for me, but I wouldn't know about it for several years. As I was packing my treasures to take to Montclair State College in 1964, my mother noticed that I was packing my two swimming trophies. She told me, "You know, they're worthless—you might as well use them for toilet paper holders."

I was confused. "No, I won them at the Laurel swimming meet in 1961." She went on to say that Sue had asked her daughters, Sharon and Toni, both champion swimmers, not to enter the meet so I would have a better chance to win. I was crushed, not for what Sue DeMoulin had done, but for what my mother said. I told her that they still meant something to me and put them in the box.

Mrs. DeMoulin maintained her friendship with my mother, but she was extraordinarily kind to me, a guardian angel.

Mrs. Dorothy L. McLaren

Librarian, Baker Jr. High School
Corpus Christi, Texas (1959-1961)

1959. Twelve years old. Baker Junior High allowed students in eighth and ninth grade to work either in the office or the library instead of taking physical education. I hated physical education. I didn't play team sports well. I was the type that was always selected last by the team captain. Being a library girl was an attractive prospect.

We worked in the library one hour a day and after school. If you worked after school you earned points toward attending the Texas Assistant Librarian Association convention. This was perfect for me. I cheerfully stayed after school and racked up enough points to attend the convention in Houston and stay at the Shamrock Hilton.

When I came back from the convention, I still was working almost everyday after school. Mrs. "Mac." told me that I didn't have to come in every day. I told her that I liked the work, and it allowed me to go home a little later, about the time my dad would arrive from work. I knew what I was hinting about, but Mrs. Mac. didn't press me for information.

Eventually, I did start talking about my mother, not to tattle, but to seek counsel on how I might better get along with her. She gave me some useful hints. I should ask if there were any chores to do before sitting down and practicing the piano. And I shouldn't answer any questions with things that my mother could, as Mrs. Mac. called, "hang on." If I was asked if I had finished my homework, I should respond with, "I am working on my Spanish," rather than "No, it's not done."

I went through puberty in eighth grade, and things got more unpleasant. I had a moderate case of acne, and of course it would flare up before my period. No subject was considered taboo at our family dinner table.

"I see you have pimples; are you constipated, or are you near your period?" This would be in front of my father and brother. I also had heavy periods and would occasionally soil the sheets, which would infuriate her. I begged her to buy me tampons. If I used a tampon and a pad, I figured I wouldn't mess up the sheets. Her response was that tampons might rupture my hymen. I finally asked my dad for money for a record and instead bought my first box of tampons. I also suffered with menstrual cramps. Wearing nylons and heels did not compensate for the other aspects of being a woman. Sometimes I would go to bed praying that I would wake up a boy. After all, my mother treated men so much better.

As I got older, my mother's punishments were more bizarre. I didn't get grounded or have my allowance taken away like my friends. I had punishments where I couldn't practice the piano and then, when I was not prepared for my lesson, I would have to call my piano teacher and tell her that I was an insolent child and didn't deserve a lesson. My mother would listen to the call on the extension phone.

The worst thing she did to me in Texas was to take my room away from me. On the last day of school, I had to clean out my locker. Although I stuffed as much as I could in my zipper binder, I was also carrying a lot of loose papers and notebooks. I came home and just dropped my binder and books on the bed. Some of the books slid onto the floor. My mother became enraged at the sight of my scattered books and yelled at me that I did not deserve to have the room. She then started to dismantle the room. She took down the curtains; she took off the bedspreads. She took my books and games out of the room. I was left with two beds, a nightstand, and a lamp. She took everything out of the closet except my clothes.

She told me I was not to go in any other room in the house. I couldn't practice the piano. I told her that she should just give me my meals in the room, and then I would be a total prisoner. She told me that I would not act the martyr. I would come to the dinner table but not be allowed to talk. My dad later intervened on the "no talking" prohibition.

"Lillian, isn't this a little severe?"

I was not allowed to phone anyone or receive any phone calls. My mother couldn't find a place for my bookcase, so she took my books out and put some of my dad's books in my bookcase and put it back in my room

Desperate for something to do, I looked at the books that were in the bookcase. I found my dad's college algebra textbook. My brother smuggled me some paper and a pencil. I went through the first few chapters. I got as far as two unknowns. We had a dachshund, and I would sneak him into the room, sit on the floor with him in my lap, and just pet him repeatedly.

My mother didn't empty out the sewing drawer in the nightstand when she dismantled my room. In it were needles, thread, and scissors. I looked at the scissors and just started saying the word "scissors" over and over again. I found that after saying the word "scissors" repeatedly, the word became meaningless. I then realized that I had been "away" briefly. I did this repeatedly while I was banished to my room. (I thought I had been meditating, but I later found out that I was dissociating.)

I also dabbled with self-injury. I would thread a needle and slip the needle between the top two layers of my skin. The rule of my game was that if I struck blood, I had to quit. It took me several days before I had all ten fingers threaded together. I also tried puncturing my leg with a straight pin. The puncture hurt, but since I was a strong swimmer and had rock solid muscles, inserting the pin further did not. There was no use in repeating that.

Fortunately for me, Jeanne Young, my mother's friend from Dallas, was visiting Corpus Christi. Jeanne asked if I could baby-sit her two boys, and I got my room back; however, it did not come without receiving a final, public insult.

While I had been banished to my room, I wrote in very small print in the back corner of the sewing drawer, "I don't like my mother, I dislike my mother, I hate my mother, I despise my mother, I loathe my mother."

My mother was always inspecting our drawers and closets. She made me give her the key to a jewelry box that I received as a gift. "In this house there will be no secrets from me." Of course, she found hat I had written. While I was entertaining the boys in my room, my mother walked back to my bedroom with Jeanne and said, "Jeanne, I want to show you what Cynthia wrote about me." She opened the drawer and let Jeanne read those five lines and then said, "Isn't that funny? Don't you think she is terribly neurotic?" Jeanne muttered, "Oh, Lill, it's probably just adolescence."

In 1960, my Uncle Victor and Aunt Vickie (my mother's sister) drove from Chicago to Corpus Christi in his new four-passenger Thunderbird. He wanted to go to Mexico and invited my parents. I thought it was a wonderful idea. I suggested to Mother that we could have Francie, our cleaning lady, stay with us since school was in session. My dad liked Victor and wanted to go on the trip. But, my mother said, no, that she needed to stay with Charles. However, I should go with them to Mexico since I could speak a little Spanish. We visited Monterey and Horse Tail Falls and had a pleasant time. On a stretch between Alice, Texas, and the US border, we hit one hundred miles per hour in his new Thunderbird.

I was only in eighth grade; I was the innocent one, but I wished that I had never gone on that trip. Mother was a hellion when we got back. She had set it up so she could make me the traitor and herself the martyr. She kept questioning me about what happened on the trip. (Yes, I spent some time with Dad, but I also spent an afternoon shopping with Vickie. Yes, Dad and I shared a bedroom, but I would go to bed, and he would go out to a bar with Victor. Sometimes he would come in at two or three in the morning.)

I was in ninth grade and knew that even though I was at Baker Junior High, this was the start of my high school grades. I was an excellent math student. In seventh grade I had been selected for a citywide, weeklong program on binary math. But, with the eroding home situation, I began to get stressed, and it was difficult to keep up my homework.

As a librarian assistant, I had access to the textbook storage closets, and those closets also had the teacher's texts: the ones with all the answers. The first time I used the teacher's copy of the algebra textbook it was just to compare an answer. I promised myself that I would only compare. (Any addicts reading this?) But I soon was using the book as a source for work I hadn't done. One day, I opened the book, and there was, a card with "To thine own self be true" written on it. I recognized Mrs. Mac.'s penmanship. I was mortified. About a week later I talked with her. She acted understanding but firm. She also said that I had to talk with my algebra teacher. I told her that I couldn't. It would be too much.

"Cynthia, you need to do this." One day after school, while I was working in the library, she and my algebra teacher entered the back part of the library, via the teachers' lounge. I don't know if he knew beforehand what I had done, but he knew it was serious. I told him what I did, and that I was very sorry. He asked me how long it had been going on. I told him about three weeks. He told me that I had to write out all the homework for those weeks, and that it would cost me one letter grade. That quarter I received a B in algebra, my favorite class.

Mrs. Mac. never mentioned the incident again, nor did I. When I left Texas in 1961, some of my school friends gave me a party and Mrs. M. was there. She gave me a dictionary that I still have. We corresponded several times while I was in Argentia, but then I lost track of her.

Mrs. McLaren was one of my guardian angels. With the pressures of living through a very troubled adolescence, I've done some things that I am not proud of, but after that, cheating wasn't one of them.

Mrs. Jopi Bannink

Neighbor, Corpus Christi, Texas (1958-1961)

1961. Fourteen years old. We were moving from Corpus Christi, Texas, to Argentia, Newfoundland, Canada, via a two-month stay in Patuxent River, Maryland. We were to stay six weeks in transient quarters in Patuxent River while my dad learned how to fly the radar belly-dome, four-engine, tripletail C-131 Constellation aircraft. This would be followed by a two-year tour of duty at Argentia in fully furnished base housing.

This meant that moving our goods involved three shipments: a small household shipment to Argentia, a larger shipment to "dead storage" (dead storage denoted that the goods could only be retrieved with a new set of orders), and the stuff we would take to Patuxent. The logistics were somewhat tricky: The bedroom furniture and the couch were destined for dead storage; the piano and vacuum cleaner were headed for Argentia. My mother had been carefully packing a large trunk with all the bedding, linens, silverware, and pillows that were to go to Argentia. The trunk was in the master bedroom.

On the day that all the packers and movers came, my mother received a telephone call from the base. One of my dad's friends had flown in from Patuxent and asked if there was anything he could take back to Patuxent. She said, yes, the television and the typewriter. She left me in charge of the packing and movers while she made the one-hour round trip to the base.

The packers came, and the movers for the dead storage shipment arrived. I went around the house and showed them which furniture was to go to dead storage. During that time, a few of my friends came over with a farewell gift: two records, the sound tracks from "The Apartment" and "Exodus," and a lovely scrapbook which was engraved with my name. We chatted and made promises that we would write to each other forever. I was not actively supervising the moving activity and did not notice that the dead-storage movers picked up the trunk with all the bed stuff for Argentia.

My mother came back and didn't immediately notice the absence of the trunk. (The movers for the shipment to Argentia were coming the next day.) She was outside watering her flowers when all of a sudden she burst into my room and screamed, "Where is the trunk?" I walked into their bedroom and saw that it wasn't there. I said, "I am so sorry, maybe it can be retrieved." She started screaming that it was gone, and it was all my fault. Of course, I had made a terrible mistake, but she was violently out of control.

She went into the kitchen and took out a large butcher knife and started chasing me. At this time there was very little furniture in the living room. I had no place to hide. I ran straight to my room. I couldn't lock the door, because she had removed the locks on our bathroom and bedroom doors. I was taller and stronger than she was and kept the door closed with my body weight braced against the door. Then she took the knife and rapidly slid it back and forth under the door. I had to move my feet around to avoid her slashing my feet, but as I did that, I was losing control of the door. All the while she was screaming, "You open the door, now!" I felt that if I did open the door, she would have stabbed me.

Then the doorbell rang. I remember praying, "Oh, please God, let it be some one who knows Mother."

It was Jopi Bannink, who lived across the street and was good friends with my mother. The Banninks had lived all around the world, and Jopi taught my mother how to cook some Indonesian dishes. My mother was still screaming even after she had opened the door to let Jopi inside.

"I'm going to kill her, I'm going kill her!" I then heard Jopi say, "Lillian, of course you are very angry, but she didn't do it on purpose...she made a mistake."

My mother started to calm down. I couldn't hear the conversation too well, but the tone assured me that it was safe to walk out to the living room. As I walked toward the living room, Jopi was facing me, but my mother's back was to me. Jopi gave me a very concerned look, and then my mother turned around.

I walked in and told them how dreadfully sorry I was that I had made such a terrible mistake. My mother was calmer, and since she now had a guest, went back to her almost charming self.

Jopi stayed until my brother came back, and I felt I was somewhat safe. My mother never apologized. For me, she had crossed the Rubicon. She had pulled my hair, slapped me, given me a black eye, but she had never picked up a weapon.

Aftermath: My mother was rarely able to forgive and forget. When we got to Argentia, she repeatedly let me know that she now had to buy linens and blankets because of my stupid mistake. She bought two English woolen blankets, one for my brother's bedroom and one for their bedroom. For my room she gave me an army cocoon-type sleeping bag. The sleeping bag did not have a zipper, and I had to shimmy to get into it. The sleeping bag was designed for about twenty degrees below zero, and therefore I spent the night alternately roasting in it or freezing on top of it. Since she was always inspecting our rooms, she also had to look at the ugly army-green sleeping bag. I guess this offended her aesthetic sense, and she sewed a pretty coverlet for the bag.

The worst thing about the bag was that it precluded me from having overnight guests. "How can you have a guest, when you don't have proper bedding?" One Friday a friend came over, and with my friend standing next to me, I asked my mother if she could spend the night. My mother gave me her typical stare which read, "You know the answer is no." I then very respectfully and very cheerfully said, "Helen can bring her brother's sleeping bag." I think she was caught off guard with my quick solution, and she said it was fine. Then she oozed her charm and asked Helen if she would like to stay for dinner.

Mrs. Bannink, a guardian angel, may have saved me from being wounded or worse.

Miss Judith G.

Physical Education teacher, Bristol High School, Naval Air Station, Argentia, Newfoundland, Canada (1961-1962)

During the cold war, Argentia Naval Air Station had one purpose: to support the airborne early warning squadrons. Their mission was to radar monitor all aerial activity over the north Atlantic, the route the Russians would take if they were provoked to send their bombers.

The ambiance was bleak; most of the buildings were painted grey. During the winter we had about six hours of daylight. Although the winter temperatures were not extremely low, the wind was fierce. Occasionally we would be sent home from school because the wind chill factor was forty degrees below zero, the temperature at which skin would freeze on contact.

Bob Hope's annual pilgrimage to visit the troops was an arctic tour and included Argentia. We attended the show, and of course, the jokes were written for those stationed on the base. I remember two of them.

"How desolate is Argentia? It is so desolate that no one goes AWOL (away without leave) because there is no place else to go."

"How windy is it in Argentia? It is so windy that no one can wear their hat, and therefore no one knows who to salute."

1961. Fifteen years old. Miss G. was my physical education and health instructor during my sophomore year. When we arrived in Argentia we stayed in the Bachelor Officers' Quarters (BOQ) on the base. The unmarried teachers also lived in the same building. The BOQ was built by the Air Force and was called the Argentia Hilton. For a desolate base, it was swank. It had ten floors, two dining rooms, a bowling alley, a snack bar, regular bar, and a gym.

Our family stayed in the BOQ for six weeks before we were assigned base housing. Besides seeing Miss G. in school, I would also cross her path at the BOQ. My dad had his first two-week deployment to Iceland while we were living there. My mother was worried about my father's twelve-hour long flights, and she was generally unhappy having not much to do. Things were getting tense, and so I stayed away from our tenth-floor rooms as much as I could.

The bar had a piano, but since I was under age I could only practice while the bar was empty. The minute someone ordered a drink, I had to leave. I would walk across to the bowling alley and bowl a few games. The pins were set manually, and the pinsetters would cheer me on. One evening while all alone, I bowled a 176.

I thought Miss G. was pretty cool. She occasionally wore her University of Michigan sweatshirt and made references to classical music. One evening when both the bar and the bowling alley were off limits to me, she invited me to her room to chat. She had this wonderful collection of classical records. She introduced me to Beethoven symphonies and piano concertos. I remember she ironed her blouses while listening to Richard Rodgers' Victory at Sea. She told me her sister was a pianist and had gone to the Interlochen Music Camp during one summer.

She asked me why I was in the lobby of the BOQ so frequently. I didn't go into details but intimated that I had a poor relationship with my mother. In school she never showed me any favoritism. I was an awful athlete. The only game I played well was volleyball. I had a strong serve but never knew where the ball would land. Health was another story. I liked science and aced all her tests. I swam quite well and was on the base swimming team. Once Judy came down to the base swimming pool and timed me. It was the fastest I had ever swum the fifty-yard freestyle—thirty-three seconds.

Finally, we got our own quarters, 1019-C, overlooking Argentia Bay. My mother had started entertaining as a way of occupying her time and invited people over for cocktails and dinner. I asked her if she could invite Judy and her roommate, who was my brother's sixth-grade teacher. My mother had the dinner party with Miss G., her roommate, and one other couple.

Miss Judith G.

For my mother's dinner parties, I served dinner and did the dishes. I did not participate in any way. Sometime during the dinner, Miss G. said that I was a lovely girl, that I was smart, had a strong sense of values, and she didn't think that I had to be so rigidly controlled.

Well, talk about a quick ticket to hell. First my mother lashed into me, "What have you told her about me?" But worse, she would tear apart Judy any chance she could get.

"You know, teachers that volunteer for teaching positions aboard military bases are probably psychological misfits." If she would see Judy at the commissary (food store) or Navy Exchange (general store), she would tell me, "I saw Judy, and she is really getting fat," or if I was with her, "Don't you think that Judy needs a haircut?" or "You know, there's a rumor that Judy is sleeping with one of the officers."

It was hard to ignore all those cutting comments. My dad was going to be in Iceland for three months during the summer of 1962. I told Judy that I didn't want to spend the summer dodging my mother. Judy suggested that I try out for the Interlochen Music Camp, and she wrote a beautiful recommendation. My dad encouraged me to "give it a try." My mother nixed the idea. "You're not going anywhere, and how do you think that we could pay for it?" (Grandparents, aunt?)

Judy kept asking me if I had sent in the application. I lied and told her that I had, perhaps it got lost at the Fleet Post Office. (All our mail was addressed to us via a F.P.O. Box in New York City.) But the truth was that it was less painful to lie about sending it in, rather than be accepted at Interlochen and not be able to go.

I never really got to say good-bye to Judy other than at the farewell party we gave all the high school teachers who were heading back to the states, but when she left I felt a void.

At this juncture one might be wondering---where was my father during these years? Where was his support for me and why didn't he intervene? The answer distills down to two reasons.

First, he depended on my mother to be a good military wife and manage our frequent moves. My mother moved thirty-seven times during my father's twenty-eight year career. (That alone would probably send many to the funny farm.) She also was responsible for the home front while he was away. He first saw my brother when Charles was six months old. He also expected my mother to be a good hostess, and sometimes that wasn't easy.

When we were in Coronado, California, my dad was the executive officer (second in command) of the squadron. After a change in command ceremony there was a reception at the officers' club, and the wife of the new commanding officer told my mother, "Honey, we are from Missouri, and I don't drink, so the entertaining will fall on your shoulders."

My mother was livid, and she really laid into my dad. This was one of the few times I heard my parents argue. "Am I really supposed to be the squadron's hostess? We live in a small two bedroom house with a tiny living and dining room. I have an eleven year old daughter and a seven year old son who are forced to share a bedroom, and you expect me to entertain the squadron just because alcohol interferes with her morals?"

But my mother did it. My dad would call on a Friday afternoon and say that he had invited a few officers and their wives for cocktails and dinner. My mother would throw soup and noodles together and make a gourmet meal, and my dad would play jazz piano. Everybody liked coming to their parties.

Our stay in Argentia, Newfoundland, was during the middle of the cold war. In fact the Cuban missile crisis of 1962 occurred while we were stationed there. My dad was a plane patrol commander and flew radar reconnaissance flights around Iceland. During the crisis the naval air station was on red alert, and the squadrons were flying double barriers. The spoken reason was to improve the efficiency of the radar tracking. The unspoken reason was, that if one of the planes were shot down, the other could continue the mission. Every time the phone rang at night my mother would freeze. My mother was not only worried about his safety, but she worried about hers. (What better way to stop radar surveillance than by attacking the base where the planes were maintained.) She wanted to take us and go back to Chicago. My dad was very patient with her. He told her he loved her, and he needed her to stay.

Secondly, my dad's older sister, who also played the piano, was institutionalized for mental illness. She joined the Army during World War II, and because she was smart, was selected for work in intelligence. She couldn't handle the stress and was given a medical discharge. She came home and started acting irrationally and also started drinking. I don't know how ill she was. (In those days if two Lithuanian doctors certified that you were certifiable, away you went.) But I do know that she died in a mental facility.

Overall, my father had an untenable position. If he came to my aid, that would enrage my mother, and she would take it out on me. However, if he did nothing, that would give my mother license to further mistreat me. She would say, "Your father is not saying anything, because he knows that you are wrong and I am right."

My father always supported my music. Many times it was he who bought my recital dresses and attended my recitals. After one recital my dad and I went for ice cream. When we got home, my mother asked us why we were late. I told her that we had gone out. My mother was upset, and she said that we should have come home and picked her up before celebrating. Trying to save the day, my dad suggested that we all go out to dinner. She said it was too late and declined. The celebration of my recital had ruined the rest of her day.

However, he knew I was hurting, and when my mother was out of the house he frequently would give me this spiel: "Both your mother and I love you very much. Try not to anger her. Please try your very best to not rock the boat. Just do well in school. I will pay for your college education, and you never have to come home again."

There were three reasons our relationship deteriorated in Argentia. First, I was older, a sophomore and junior in high school, and I was involved with extra curricular activities which kept me away from home. If she was angry at me, she would start to stew over what I did wrong during the day, and then when I came home in the evening, I'd be attacked for some misdemeanor.

The second reason was that my father was away two weeks out of every six. During those two weeks he would be flying barrier flights around Iceland, and my mother was always worried that he would crash.

The third reason why our relationship deteriorated was where we living—on a remote and isolated base.

For kids, living on the base in Argentia was like living in a theme park. We could use the base transportation, go to a movie for a dime, bowl a line for a quarter, and have lunch for less than a dollar. On the weekend we could spend the afternoon at the pool or in the gym. For the military it was demanding and stressful duty. For wives it was a virtual prison.

Most offshore orders landed a family in a foreign country, and therefore wives could immerse themselves in learning the language and the culture. (My mother had a ball while living in Japan.) In Argentia, there was really no place to go if you left the base.

The surrounding fishing towns could be visited, but the area was rather impoverished. Because Newfoundland had a high rate of tuberculosis, no one was supposed to drink milk or eat anything prepared locally. St. John, the picturesque capital, was ninety miles from Argentia, but the first forty-five miles was gravel road. Our family visited St. John only once, and the round trip took us eight hours.

The Navy did show some sympathy for the wives. On most Fridays, Eloise, the twin engine DC-3 plane that brought in our mail and vegetables from the states, flew kids for their orthodontist appointments and wives to St. John for a day away from the base. Although my mother was married to a pilot, she was deathly afraid of flying. We encouraged her to have a day away from Argentia, but she never went. Some women just drank and played bridge to kill time, and sadly some women cracked under the stress and had to be flown back to the states in a straight-jacket. It didn't matter how severe the mental distress was; that was military procedure.

My mother occupied her time by baking cakes and giving dinner parties, reading Freud, and finding ways to make me miserable. She succeeded at all three.

While we were stationed in Corpus Christi, we lived in the city. My mother could yell at me, and no neighbor would be aware of us fighting. When we moved to Argentia, my mother needed to take a different approach.

Our quarters in Argentia had been hastily built during the cold war to meet the needs of the military dependents. The exterior walls were well insulated to protect us from Argentia's severe weather, but the walls between each of the quarters were paper thin. We could hear our neighbors on both sides. This meant my mother couldn't yell at me.

She started lecturing. I was verbally assaulted for normal things that got teens in trouble, picking on my brother, procrastinating doing my homework, or dressing sloppily. But I also got lengthy lectures on some misdemeanor I had committed and on my innate personality. By this time she had read several books by Freud and was dishing that out as well. I had penis envy of my brother, I wanted a romantic relationship with my father, I was a narcissist because I would spend hours at the piano, and because I didn't have any compassion for her, I was sadistic.

Initially these lectures would either whittle me down to a blubbering mess or anger me enough to say, "I hate you," after which she would respond, "You hate me? I wish I'd never had you!" and then I would storm away. I remember being harshly affected by these lengthy lectures. But I soon picked up the signal that her lectures weren't as much to discipline me, but to break me down. I developed another defensive strategy: I would show no emotion and she would not make me angry or cry. Admittedly, my initial efforts at being stoic failed, and she would make me cry or yell hateful responses. But soon I was able to stand through an entire lecture and not say anything or show any emotional response. I would even play a game to divert myself from fully listening to her. I called it, "Insults Baseball."

She would lecture me, and I would be listening and waiting for each of her well worn insults. "And this reminds me of the time when you were seven that you did this to your brother. You are jealous of your brother."(Good start, mother, you're on first base.) She would continue on and then say, "You know, you are your own worst enemy." (Nice going, mother, you made second base.) "Everybody has their cross to bear and you are mine." (Good going, mother, you made it to third. I wonder what's going to get you to home plate. Oh---here it comes.) "You are standing there silent; you hate me. Well I want you to know that I hate you more; I wish I'd never had you." (Hurray for mom, you got to home plate.)

One of the problems living and dealing with my mother in Argentia was her unpredictability. In Texas, I was under her thumb. She could vent her frustrations regularly by yelling, pulling my hair, cursing, and ridiculing me. It surely wasn't pleasant, but I usually could sense her mood and experienced what I expected.

We had a party-line phone system, and we shared the party line with our next-door neighbor. Our time to make and receive calls was from the hour to the half, and our neighbor's time was the half-hour to the hour. If someone needed to interrupt a call, the phone made an audible click, letting one know that the other party had lifted the receiver. We had a large electric clock on the wall above the telephone so we could carefully monitor our calls.

One evening, I got a call from a friend at eight twenty-five. She hadn't written down the geometry homework. I went upstairs to retrieve my notebook but couldn't immediately find the assignment. I finished the call around eight thirty-two. If our neighbor had picked up the phone at eight thirty, I wouldn't have heard the "click" because I was running around looking for the assignment.

The next day our neighbor told my mother that I had been on the phone on her half hour as she tried to make a call around eight forty. My mother asked me if I had been on the phone past the half hour, and I said that I hung up at exactly eight thirty-two. She questioned me, "Are you sure?" I said that I definitely was off the phone by eight thirty-five. I apologized, but I surely was expecting that I would be punished, lose phone privileges, and receive a lengthy lecture. I was braced for the worst, and then she said, "Well, she was probably drunk...you know she is an alcoholic."

On another day I came home after a long SCUBA practice, and my mother met me at the door. She was holding a fork and asked,

"Do you know what this is?"

"Well, I believe it's a four-tined fork."

"Don't you dare talk back to me!"

"I'm sorry, did I forget to wash it?"

"Oh, you washed it. It was in the dish drainer, but the fork is greasy."

"I'm sorry, I'll rewash it."

"You think it's that easy. I just don't know...we give you piano lessons and put braces on your teeth, and you can't be responsible enough to properly wash the dinner dishes?"

"I'll be more careful next time."

"That's what you always say, but do you change your bad habits? No—because you don't really care about anything except your SCUBA course and piano. Why are you sitting down?"

"Because I'm very tired, and I know this is going to be a long lecture."

"You stand up now. I'll tell you when you can sit down."

"Mother, what do you want me to do? Do you want me to rewash all the dishes?"

"Why should you rewash the dishes when it's only one greasy fork?"

"Exactly."

"You think you are so smart, don't you. Well this is going to cost you plenty. Why are you just standing there? Oh, you're going to go silent on me, because you hate me. Get out of here, you're a G.D.S.O.B.G.F.N. (Goddamn, son of a bitch, good for nothing), and I wish I'd never had you."

I had no mentors in my junior year. I just stayed very busy. I would take the station bus to school at seven fifteen in the morning instead of the school bus at eight. After school, I would go to swim practice, and then with wet hair, I would go to the naval base chapel and practice the organ. (I was the organist for the early Protestant service.) I would take the station bus back to our quarters and come home about eight in the evening. I would eat dinner with my eyes shut due to the chlorine irritation. I would work the daily cryptogram and go to bed. I would wake up at four in the morning and do my homework.

That schedule basically kept me out of harm's way, but what usually followed was that I was so exhausted that I would make mistakes on the weekend. I would forget to do this or do that poorly. Then the lectures would follow. Sometimes I would sit on the stairs for an hour (I would time her), and she would continue to drone her child rearing philosophies and my faults.

"Children are such a sacrifice; I wish I never had you. I read Freud cover to cover, because I thought something was wrong with me, and I found out that what's wrong—is you. Why can't you be more like your brother? You are your own worst enemy. Everybody has a cross to bear, and you're mine. You have no compassion for anyone."

One of the ways my mother attacked me was by both assaulting my friends and my selection of friends. On an offshore military base, children of enlisted personnel, chief petty officers, officers, and civilians all attended the same school. Rate or rank did not make a difference; only brains and grades did. My two closest girl friends, Helen and Linda, were the daughters of chief petty officers, and we had a lot of fun together. We studied together, dreamed about our futures together, and bemoaned the fact that we were social wallflowers.

Once I came home from a sleep over at Linda's house, and my mother said, "You know there is something wrong with you. You don't have any officers' children as friends."

"I like Linda and Helen. We have a lot in common. We do well in school, don't like hanging out at the base teen club, and we are all musicians."

"Well, I just think that it's peculiar that you don't have any other friends. Perhaps it's that you're sub-optimal and the officers' friends don't want to mix with you."

"Maybe you're right. I don't know."

Aftermath: There were eleven juniors in my high school. The top student was the son of a chief petty officer. Then came our trio. A captain's daughter married the biology teacher at the end of the year, and the commanding officer of the base's daughter had to visit her grandmother for an "emergency vacation." Helen, Linda, and I not only finished college, but we went on to graduate study. I received my M.S. in biology from the Illinois Institute of Technology in 1977. I defended my thesis when I was five months pregnant.

During my junior year, I was invited to take the US Navy SCUBA training course. I easily qualified for the swimming part and studied hard for the academic part, learning about compressed gases, the bends, and nitrogen narcosis. Then came the snorkeling exercises. This first part took about two months to complete.

In the third month we finally got our tanks. In those days, one used double hose regulators, which meant air was always flowing and you had to learn how to stop your air as well as breathe. We practiced all the skills, clearing out masks, diving in the pool wearing the tanks, retrieving our tanks from the bottom of the pool, and buddy breathing. I'd sit at the bottom of the pool and play metallic checkers getting used to breathing from the tank.

Then came the final certification, the "panic test." My mother said she wasn't interested in being there; I said I understood. It would be noisy and confusing. There were several of us who were going to be challenged that evening, and everybody brought their friends to cheer them on. It would not be a serene event. My mother showed up shortly before I started my test.

I had two instructors in the water following me, and I made sure that I kept my eyes on them so I would know where they were. Suddenly, my mask was ripped off my face, and my air was turned off. A third instructor had dived into the pool. I found my mask but couldn't turn on my air. I broke the surface without my mask and air on. I had panicked. The first words out of my mother's mouth were, "I knew you'd fail!"

In the spring of my junior year, my ego gave out, bacteria invaded my lungs, and I was hospitalized with pneumonia. My parents came to my hospital room the next day, and my mother bounced in with the jubilant news that Judy G. had flown to Norfolk, Virginia, to ask an officer to marry her since she was pregnant with his child. After they left, I broke down and cried. A nurse came in to check on me, and I yelled at her to just stay away. The doctor on duty came and asked me what was wrong. I remember answering, "What is right?" I then apologized for being flip and said that I was feeling sorry for myself since I would be missing a week of school.

Miss Judith G.

I am thankful for knowing Judy. She may not have saved me from my mother's wrath. She had to be careful in her relationship with me since we were living on a military base, a very closed environment. But, on a small scale she intervened on my behalf, and I appreciated her efforts.

Judy qualifies as a guardian angel in my book. I especially enjoyed our conversations in the BOQ and her introducing me to classical music records. When I got back to the states, I started my own record collection. One other thing: She said I had the potential to attend a school like the University of Michigan. Those were sweet words.

Mr. Stephen T.
Band director, Sparta High School
Sparta, New Jersey (1963-1964)

1963. Seventeen years old. I arrived at Sparta High School early in October about a month after school started. It didn't faze me in the least. I was smart, and I knew I would adapt even though this was the third of three high schools that I had attended.

To avoid going home right after school dismissal, I would practice the piano in one of the practice cubicles in the band room. Mr. T. thought I was pretty good and asked me if I knew how to play the glockenspiel. ("What's a glockenspiel?") I found out it was a portable xylophone used in the marching band. I said, "Sure." I marched in the band for the rest of the football band season, had a uniform, and a group of new friends.

I told Mr. T. that I was interested in studying music in college. He suggested that I take music theory the next semester, which he taught. I don't think I ever confided in him about my mother. I may have mentioned that she was very strict; that's about it. However, I frequently talked about Mr. T. to my parents. Mr. T. arranged for a group of interested music students to go to New York City. I heard Leonard Bernstein conduct Shostakovich's Symphony No. 5. It is a performance I will never forget.

Mr. T. came to my aid in a big way one spring day in 1964. My mother was supposed to take me for my driver's test, and it was arranged that she would meet me at a designated time in front of the school. The evening before we had carefully figured out after which class I would need to leave school.

When I got to school, I found that the schedule had been changed to assembly schedule. That meant that if my mother arrived at the designated time, I would be twenty minutes late. I went to the office and asked if I could use the phone to notify my mother of the change. They had strict rules in those days. No phone calls unless it was an illness or death. I pleaded my case, "My mother will be angry if I am late." No deal.

By the time I walked out to the car, she had been waiting about twenty-five minutes. She was furious. I don't remember what she said, but she was railing at me. I told her that it wasn't my fault, I didn't know about the assembly, and furthermore, I could not contact her. She did not listen to me at all. I finally yelled that I didn't need the driver's license, got out of the car, and slammed (really slammed) the door. I walked back into school. I did not realize that she had gotten out of the car and followed me.

Knowing that Mr. T. did not have a class that period, I walked into the band room just to calm myself before going to the office and requesting a late pass. I heard the vice-principal call my name. "Will Cynthia Kanapicki report to the front office," came over the PA system. I knew then that my mother was in the building. A friend of mine burst into Mr. T's room and asked him if he had seen me because my mother was on a rampage.

I became frightened and asked Mr. T. to hide me.

"You've got to hide me. She could do anything."

Mr. T spent not a second trying to persuade me that it couldn't be that bad. He said, "Don't hide in the practice rooms, she'll look there. Hide in the uniform closet, there behind my desk." I hid in the closet and waited, and then I heard her come in.

"Where is she? I know she's in here!"

I heard Mr. T. say, "Look, she's not here. You can check in the practice rooms. She's not here."

At which point my mother said, "If I find out that you've been hiding her, you are in big trouble." Then she left. I didn't leave the closet for a while, frightened that she might zip right back into the band room and catch me.

Finally the school bell rang, and I went to my last class. In those days the regular buses left after school, the activity bus left at four thirty, and the athletes left at six o'clock. I went home with the jocks. I didn't know what to expect, and I feared the worst. When I got home, she said absolutely nothing. Nothing. Meanwhile, the whole school now knew that I had a nutcase for a mother.

After high school graduation, I kept in contact with Mr. T. We had moved from a rented house to a home we bought which was a few houses down from his. His wife was a nurse and worked during the summer when Mr. T. had a lighter schedule. Mr. T. asked me to baby-sit his two daughters a few times. My mother thought that it was rather inappropriate that I baby-sit for him, since I might be alone in the house with him. When he asked me to baby-sit again and I declined, I confided in him about her irrational behaviors.

He asked me what I was going to do during the summer. I told him, "Mostly try to stay out of uniform closets." He asked me if I played any other instruments. I told him that I also played the organ. I remember him saying, "No, I mean real instruments like a trumpet or a clarinet." (Reader, you may chuckle.) I told him that I had always wanted to learn how to play the French horn because the sound was so beautiful.

The summer before starting at Montclair State College, I participated in Sparta's beginning band program. Almost every other student was in elementary school, and there I sat—a high school graduate. But, I had fun learning the French horn, and the program lasted a few hours each day, which was enough to get me out of the house legally.

As it turned out, that summer band program turned out to be a real gift. In college, I started out as a piano major and vocal minor, but I received a "C" on my voice jury and was asked to select a different minor instrument. I became a French horn minor. I was able to study with Kathleen Wilbur who played for the New York City Ballet.

Although I was initially devastated by the quasi-failure, it turned out I really had the best of both worlds. I was a piano major and still could sing in the choir, but I also could play in the band and orchestra. My learning the French horn led me to meeting Diane T., my off-campus roommate, and my husband who also plays the French horn.

Yes, Mr. Steve T., you were a guardian angel.

Dr. Gerald Edwards

Football coach, Health education professor,
Montclair State College, New Jersey (1965)

1965. Eighteen years old. During the second semester of my freshman year, I needed to take health education as part of the requirements for my education degree. I remember finding out that the course was taught by the football coach and expected that the class would surely be a bust. I asked one of the upperclassmen about Dr. Edwards, and she told me that I was very lucky. It might be one of the best courses I would take.

She was right. From the minute he stepped into our class, he took control of the course. He had a terrific smile and a winning personality. We launched into discussions about sex education, adolescence, peer pressure, everything. He was the type of teacher that had students just begging him for a few minutes of his time after class. While his football players were practicing, he would sit in the bleachers and do informal counseling. I stood in line like a lot of the other freshmen.

I told him about not getting along with my mother, and that I didn't want to spend the summer at home, but I didn't think I had too many alternatives. He asked me a few questions, and when he found out I could swim well, he suggested that I get my Red Cross Water Safety Instructor's certificate and teach swimming at a summer camp. I took his advice and enrolled in a month-long course at the Summit YMCA and completed the training. I applied for a job through the Quincy, Massachusetts YMCA and got a job on Cape Cod as a general counselor with swimming proficiency. But my mother was not happy with my decision-making or my plans, and she let me know it. Things at home quickly deteriorated during the spring.

I felt that I had consumed my informal counseling minutes with Dr. Edwards, but I was hungry for more. One evening, I started to walk in the general direction of his house.

I made it a game. He lived in Caldwell just over the ridge. I knew his address, but I didn't know where he lived, so I would walk a certain distance and then turn back. State-school-run dormitories had strict rules. A freshman only had twenty late hours. You had to sign out. You had to sign in. I would make sure I got back by one in the morning when the dorm closed. I was a social zero and had only used a few of my late hours. Each time I would start walking to his house, I would walk a little farther and get a little closer, but, of course, it would be riskier to get back on time.

Finally, I found his house. I would stay across the street and just watch his house. Then I would start the trip back to reach the dorm before one.

I confided in a sophomore dorm-mate what I was doing. I told her, that in a strange way, standing in front of his house made me feel better. One Sunday, when I was about to walk to Caldwell, she asked me where I was going. I told her, "Caldwell" and she said, "Why don't we go with you?"

"You mean we're all going to walk to Caldwell? You're kidding. Are we hobbits? No, I am going alone." And then she, who would later go on to get a Ph.D. in clinical psychology, said, "We all go, or I tell the dorm resident director." So we all marched off on my yellow brick road to Caldwell. When we reached Dr. Edwards's home, he cheerfully invited us in. I sat there thinking, yes, I am sitting in his house now, but this is surreal. Dr. Edwards kindly drove us back to the dorm. Unfortunately, being inside his house with three dorm mates didn't quite provide the emotional "fix" I craved.

It was a Monday night at the end of the spring term, and I had just performed in a band concert. Most of my friends were going to West's Diner to hang out. We just had exams to go through; I would be home within two weeks. I remember feeling terribly lost and not connected to anything. I ostensibly had a job, but I didn't even know if I could or even wanted to go. But going home loomed ahead of me as the greatest problem, because there was going to be a two-week stay before I left for camp, if indeed I could go.

On that fateful evening I didn't stop in my dorm, and I didn't sign out at the front desk. I just started walking to Caldwell. The trip took longer than usual since I was wearing heels, and by the time I got there my feet were blistered, and I was exhausted. Still, I stood outside across the street in front of his house until his house lights went out. I looked at my watch; it was about twelve thirty in the morning. There was no way I could get back to the dorm on time, and at that point I really didn't care.

I walked to a nearby elementary school and sat down in a swing. I just sat there immobilized, not afraid of what might happen to me, or concerned about what rules I had broken. The passage of time has blurred many memories, but I remember as I was sitting in that swing, that I was no longer in control of what I was doing. A police car drove by, and I made no attempt to hide from view. It was as if I was just letting things play out.

About two o'clock, a car stopped in front of the playground. I saw the window roll down, and I heard Dr. Edwards say, "Cynthia, get in the car." I got up from the swing and walked to his car. I got in, and he first asked me if I was all right. I said yes—but nothing else. In a deadly serious tone he told me that the college had been looking for me, that the dorm director had contacted him, and that he was driving me back to Freeman Hall. This was a different Dr. Edwards from the affable professor in health education.

The reality of what I had done, and who was driving me back to the dorm shocked me back to some state of normalcy. I was very aware of my predicament. When we arrived at the dorm, he said, "Cynthia, it is apparent that you have some serious problems; you need therapy. I can't help you, but I can refer you to someone who can." I mumbled that I heard therapy was hard, that I was weak, and lacked courage. At which point he smiled and returned to the Dr. Edwards I knew and admired.

He said, "No, I don't think so—you are a real fighter. I didn't think that I lived within walking distance of the college." I will never be able to thank him enough for saying that. He exonerated me of any guilt for that evening.

When I got back to the dorm, my first worry was whether my parents had been contacted. My sophomore friend, in whom I had confided previously, had begged the dorm director not to call my parents since my mother was known to be such a witch. I was given a list of people I had to call the next morning, but as I crawled into bed at about three o'clock in the morning, I felt very cared for.

That escapade kicked me out of the dorm and earned me three lectures from administrators. I had to see the Dean of Women, the deputy Dean of the College, and the dorm director. Each of them told me that I had not handled my problems in an adult way. This incident was on my permanent college record and did not bode well for being a future teacher. I remember listening and thinking that what they were saying had relevance but little impact. The evening before someone had shown that he cared what happened to me, and I might be better for it.

I missed my next health education class since I had all those appointments with college administrators. I did go to Dr. Edwards' class on Thursday, but actively avoided eye contact. Halfway through the hour I finally looked up and glanced at him. I don't know if there was true eye contact, but the vibes I picked up were, "It's OK."

The music department and Panzer physical education were on opposite sides of the campus, so the chance of crossing his path was minimal. But every once in a while, I would see him and make an effort to greet him.

"Hi, Dr. Edwards, how are things going?"

"Fine, how are things going with you?"

"I'm still in therapy with Dr. Hauer; it's hard, but he's great."

Dr. Edwards stayed at Montclair only one more year. Then he received an academic appointment in New York City. I am sure that he continued to serve as a guardian angel to other confused, needy students.

Dr. Herbert Hauer, Ph.D.

Clinical psychologist, Montclair State College, New Jersey, (1965-1968)

1965. Eighteen years old. Through Dr. Edwards' referral, I met and starting working with Dr. Hauer. The first time I had a session with him, he introduced himself, and then he sat down and said he had to finish something. He was typing a memo on an old Underwood typewriter with less than great technique which immediately put me at ease.

I was expecting to receive my fourth "Do You Realize What You Have Done?" lecture. Instead, he asked me how I was feeling. I told him, "A little washed out," and then I added, "You probably think I am crazy for what I did."

He responded, "No, you're not crazy, but you are expressing a need." (Dear reader, did you pick up you *are* expressing a need?" He didn't say you *were* expressing a need, and I had better get my act together, or I might flunk out.) My psyche translated, "You are expressing a need" into "I will help you." I wanted to jump in his lap.

And that was how my three-year therapeutic relationship with Dr. Hauer started. As a bonus, he was also able to override my being kicked out of the dorm. I was considered a psychological hardship case and allowed to stay in the dorm during my sophomore year.

Dr. Hauer was friendly, a little nonchalant, and extremely supportive. He gently confronted me on serious issues, but he never pressed me for information. One of the ways I survived with my mother was by being an ace liar. Frequently I would spend a session apologizing for the lies from the previous session. We developed this agreement that if he asked a question, and I felt a lie coming on, rather than lie, I was supposed to give him a cue and just not answer. Invariably, whenever I would dodge a painful question, I would come to the next session just waiting to be uncorked.

He called me a "3-B girl:" brains, beauty, and body. He encouraged me to go to mixers, "You can't live your life in a practice room," and he listened to me talk about my mother. He fortified me for the times when the dorms closed, and I had to go home. Since she didn't know I was in therapy, it was like playing a game with marked cards, but for once I had the advantage. She could be cruelly berating me and telling me all my faults: I was a neurotic musician, who was book smart but really very stupid, that I was worth nothing, and always topping if off with, "you're nothing but a G.D.S.O.B.G.F.N." I listened and endured her harangues wearing invisible armor and thinking, "God, wait until Dr. Hauer hears this."

He drove a cute Karmann Ghia convertible, and when I saw his car parked by the psychology annex, it instantly made me feel better. He encouraged me to follow through with the Quincy YMCA Camp position in Cape Cod. "If your parents don't want to drive you to Boston, take a bus!" I did spend the summer at Camp Hayward on Cape Cod and had a healthy, beautiful summer. (I also met John-John Kennedy and some of his secret service men at a carnival that Camp Burgess sponsored.)

My sophomore year, the "wise-fool" year, was almost a washout. Sophomore year was the year that students switched instruments, majors, and sometimes colleges. For me it was the year that almost broke me.

My first emotional crisis started during a three-day weekend when the college and dormitories closed, and I had to go home. However, things were a little more complicated. I couldn't leave on Friday since I was in the marching band and had to stay for a game on Saturday afternoon. The plan was that after the game I would take a bus to the Port Authority in New York City and then take a bus to Dover, New Jersey, where my mother would pick me up.

A music major, a senior percussionist, offered to drive me home since his home was also in northwest New Jersey. It was a welcome invitation since it would save me about four hours bus travel and save my mother from having to drive to Dover. I called my mother and told her that a music major was going to drive me home, and we would be arriving around seven o'clock. She said that she would make dinner. I enjoyed his conversation on the drive. He wanted to stop for coffee, and so we arrived a little later than planned. I knew that would be a little upsetting for my mother, but I didn't dwell on it. We arrived at eight. Mother served dinner and then ushered us into the living room for coffee.

I thought she would leave us alone, but she sat down, and I began to get worried. My mother starting asking him questions. I don't remember the content, but they were a bit too personal. Her next remark was, "Are you aware of the fact that jingling the change in your pocket is a substitute form of masturbation?" I froze. He stood up and said, "Well, I think it's time for me to leave."

I followed him to the door while profusely apologizing. He looked at me, said nothing, and was gone. I went upstairs and asked my mother, "Why did you say that? This wasn't a date. Even if you didn't like him, he did you a favor by driving me home." Her response, "I didn't like his attitude. Please do the dishes."

When I got back to school, I slithered around the music department. I made sure I was nowhere near the band room when the concert band practiced. I didn't practice the piano in the evening (He spent a lot of time in the music building.) and therefore was not prepared for my piano lessons. Taking piano lessons without practicing was stressful enough, but I also lied that I had practiced on the mandatory practice record. Eventually I ran into him, and I again apologized for my mother's behavior. His response was, "Don't you think she should be put away?"

Dr. Hauer got me through that episode.

The school closed again right before the child psychology midterms. This was a crucial course. Your student teaching assignment was determined in part on how well you did in your psych-ed courses. We all knew that, and I took home my child psychology book and notes. My mother asked me if I was prepared for the midterm exams. I said that I had read the material (I lied), and that I had started to study (another lie). At which point, she started quizzing me about the material. I guessed at some answers and gave wrong answers just to verbalize something. Then she pounced, "I've never been to college, but I know more about psychology than you will ever know. You haven't learned anything. You are totally unprepared. You've procrastinated, and you're going to do poorly. (Here comes one of my favorites) You are your own worst enemy."

When I got back to the dorm on Sunday, all the sophomores were burning the midnight oil studying for the midterm. I opened up my book and started to study, but I couldn't concentrate. I tried, but my mind just wandered. I just went to bed.

On the day of the exam, I picked up a test, looked at all the multiple choice questions, and realized I was going to do poorly. I wrote my name on the top, circled all the (a) answers, and turned it in. On Wednesday the professor asked to see me after class. He told me that I had indeed failed the midterm, and even if I aced the final, the best I could get would be a C. However, he went on to say that the child study was a large part of the grade, and if I did well on that, I could eke out a B. I thanked him for his generosity. I did take the final exam and got a B, but I never did the child study and therefore received an incomplete. My "I" turned into an "F" when I missed the deadline for completion of "incompletes." My cumulative GPA plummeted from a 3.4 to 2.6 in one semester.

I talked to Dr. Hauer about the midterm, the child study, and the incomplete. But, I was still on the rebound from the "jingling coins" incident. There were times in therapy I didn't want to talk about her. I told him that the time I had in therapy was precious, and sometimes I just didn't want to consume my time with crap about her. In an uncanny way, I felt that talking about her was empowering her to still control my life even in his office, in the psych building, thirty-five miles away from Sparta.

I was also having problems with my piano professor. I was not the best piano major. But, I was competitive and tried to move up the ladder. I set my goals too high and barely made it through my juries. My piano teacher was rigid and demanding. He may have been the teacher my technique required—but not my psyche.

In retrospect, Dr. Hauer could have actively nudged or even nagged me to complete the requirements for the child psychology course, but he didn't. In a way, he let me hang myself on that one, and I loved him dearly for that. It was like saying that Cynthia, the person, was more important than any course she was taking.

Aftermath: I retook child psychology in my senior year, did a decent job on my child study, and earned a B. The teacher was a child psychoanalyst from New York City and she was fascinating.

During the rest of my stay at Montclair State College, I saw Dr. Hauer about once a week. He was quite proactive. One of the problems of attending a state school was, if the college closed, so did the dorms, and I was forced to go home. This was usually accompanied by tyrannical behavior from my mother and a setback for me. I would go to the next session saying, "She hates me, and I despise her." It would take a couple of sessions for me to reach equilibrium.

He suggested that I take a job that would earn me enough money for a car, so I wouldn't have to go home when the dorms closed. During the summer of 1966 I earned $700 by working in a beer bottle factory in Wharton, New Jersey, serving as a supply organist in Sparta, and teaching private swimming lessons. My dad helped me purchase a used 1960-model Mercury for $600.

My junior year went a lot better. When the dorms closed, I visited friends and rarely visited home. This would anger my mother intensely, but I wasn't around for the shouting. I moved off campus and lived on the third floor of a large home with one roommate, Diane T. Diane was a great roommate. She was a Spanish major and played the French horn. She was very popular and dated a lot. I got to go on a few double dates with her. She lived in Pt. Pleasant. With my newly found freedom, my Mercury, we frequently headed south. Pt. Pleasant sits on the Atlantic and is sort of a mini-Atlantic City. Regardless of the weather or the season, it was always fun to visit. Diane's family had suffered a tragedy. Her six-year old brother had died of leukemia. When I visited their home, there was a palpable sadness, but even so, it was still more enjoyable than visiting mine.

In the fall of my junior year, Dr. Hauer told me that he was going away for a few months, and he wanted me to work with someone else. He referred me to an East Orange psychiatrist, Dr. Jack Chernus. I told him that I didn't need it, that I would be good, and that I wouldn't walk anywhere. But he stood pretty firm.

There was a catch: MSC was not going to pay for the therapy. He wanted to have a conference with my parents, and I told him, absolutely no. My mother might come, but she'll use it against me later, please, no. Instead, he had a conference with my father. I don't know what Dr. Hauer said to my dad, but he must have used the right approach, because I got a call from my dad telling me there was no problem: He would pay for the sessions.

Shortly after that phone call, my dad invited me to lunch in New York City. He told me that whatever I needed, if he could afford it, that I would have his full financial support. And then his eyes glazed over, and I knew that he was thinking, "I'm sorry that your relationship with your mother has led to this."

I was almost going to let him say that, but I didn't. I knew if he opened the door, I would come back with, "You don't know all the things she did to me. You don't know that she chased me around with a butcher knife, you don't know that she was always ridiculing me in public and private, and when you were in Iceland flying the barriers protecting the United States from Russia, she was in Argentia taking out her frustrations on me."

I figured that if I said those things, I would hurt my Dad in the short run and maybe myself later. I didn't know what private conversations my parents might have had about my seeing a shrink, but if my mother were to ask my Dad what I had said about her, he could honestly say, "Lillian, she said nothing."

Instead, I said, "Hey, dad, you know how you used to help pick out my recital dresses when I was younger? Well, I am going to be accompanying the Mozart Clarinet Concerto in a few months, and I would like a gorgeous black dress." We went to Lord and Taylor, and he helped me select a beautiful dress.

I went to Dr. Jack Chernus. Dr. Hauer had arranged for a ride that would get me to East Orange, but I was on my own for transportation back to the college. The first session was mostly intake: "Any psychosis in the family?" "Yes, my mother." "Medically diagnosed?" "No." "Has she ever been hospitalized?" "No" "Any organic brain disease?" "No." "Were you ever dropped on your head?" "No." I don't know what type of therapeutic approach he was using, but I hated his sessions.

Basically, he said "Hmm," on one of two pitches. He was not supportive. At the end of the first session, I went to leave through the door I came in, and he motioned that I needed to use the exit door. I remember saying, "Coming here was like going to a goddamn supermarket."

But whatever he said, or didn't say, would wreak psychic havoc on the way back to campus. After I left his office, which was situated in a tall apartment building on a classy boulevard, I had to walk across a bridge that spanned the expressway. I frequently had the urge to jump off and just splat on the highway. Instead, I would keep walking to the bus stop, take the bus, and the next one, and the next. I would get back to campus wiped out and would have missed the last dinner.

I couldn't stand the lack of interaction. I wrote a song, "It's no fun to be someone, it's so fun to be no one" (sort of a Broadway parody on Emily Dickinson's "I'm nobody, who are you?"), and I mailed it to him. The next session he handed it back to me and told me that he didn't read music. (Philistine.)

It was a miserable two months. I do remember one interesting exchange. My dad's tour of duty in New Jersey was ending, and he wasn't sure where the Navy would send him for his last pre-retirement duty. My dad considered that he would ask for something around New Jersey or New York City so my brother could complete high school in Sparta, New Jersey. My mother said that she would really like to retire in California. And this was her pitch: that I, who was so miserable at MSC, could transfer to California and live with Dad for two years. I told that to Dr. Chernus, and he looked at me and said, "You didn't fall for that, did you?" And that was the extent of my therapy from Dr. Jack Chernus.

Unfortunately, my mother found out that I was seeing a psychiatrist and also that I had been in therapy with Dr. Hauer. My dad told me he didn't tell her, but I assume that she found the checks written to Dr. Chernus. Overnight my invisible armor vanished. I stayed away as much as I could, but I couldn't avoid going home for holidays.

Eventually, she cornered me and would start her blitz. "So you've seen a psychiatrist. Did you tell him how much you hate me?" (Yes). "Does it make you feel better?" (No). "Do you realize that you are part of the problem?" (Yes). "Well, I want you to know something...everyone has their cross to bear, and you're mine." (I'm sorry). "Aren't you going to say anything?" (No)."You're just standing there; don't you have any compassion for anyone else?" (Yes, my college roommate who lost her brother). "You really are worthless, you're like Patty McCormack in the *Bad Seed*." (No, there are two therapists who think I'm worth the effort.)

In comparison to my washout sophomore year, my grades improved during my junior year. I student taught at an elementary school close to the campus. (This was a plum position, and again Dr. Hauer intervened since my grades were hardly stellar.) I found out that I really enjoyed teaching kids. By the end of the school year, I felt strong enough to live at home during the summer. I was going to teach swimming for the Lake Mohawk country club, and, more importantly, I had lined up a great piano teacher in Newark. Most of my piano major friends had studied during summers, and I, of course, had missed two summers, one at camp and one at the beer bottle factory. I had fantasies of giving a really great senior piano recital. Dr. Hauer wasn't too enthusiastic about my plans. "Have fun, go to camp, this is probably the last summer you can do this."

I arrived home in June, exhausted from the string of all-nighters I had pulled studying for final exams and writing papers. I came home with two suitcases of dirty clothes, which I left downstairs but unpacked. After arriving, I told my mother that I was exhausted and just needed to sleep for a few hours. She said she understood. I hadn't been asleep for more than an hour when she burst in my room and started screaming, "You're just like your father, you come here, eat, shit, and expect your laundry done. All the clothes in your suitcases are dirty." She slammed the door and left the house. I brought home dirty clothes—so what. I didn't ask her to unpack my suitcase nor do my laundry. I'd been home exactly two hours.

I vividly remember going into the bathroom and looking in the mirror and talking to myself out loud, "You cannot stay here this summer." I felt I looked like the wicked witch in *Snow White and the Seven Dwarfs*. I channeled my anger to action.

I tried calling Dr. Hauer, but things were shut down pretty well, even in the psych department. I called the American Camping Association and found out that a Jewish camp in Vermont needed a counselor. The next day without asking my mother's permission, I drove four hours to meet the camp directors at some oasis off the New York turnpike. I told them I was a Red Cross Certified Water Safety Instructor and had one summer of camping experience. They asked if I could play any Jewish songs on the piano. I told them, no, but I knew the music from *Fiddler on the Roof* and could dance the hora. They hired me on the spot.

I drove home and announced to my mother that I was leaving in three days. I called the country club and apologized that I couldn't teach swimming, and then I made the hardest call, the one to the piano teacher in Newark. I thought I would just say my plans had changed. But I told him up front, that my home situation was unlivable, and I would be going to work at a camp. I had never done this. I had always publicly muted my problems with my mother. I never said she was a witch, or she hated me, or she abused me. Instead, I told people that I had a poor relationship with my mother, couching it in words that told the listener, that I assumed some of the responsibility.

That summer "Up, Up and Away" was on the radio in the top something. I am not a lover of pop music, but every time I heard that song while driving to Vermont, I turned the radio full volume and belted out the words. "Would you like to ride in my beautiful balloon?" I wrote to Dr. Hauer at the University of Vermont in Burlington and told him what happened. He wrote to me while I was at camp and lauded my decision and courage.

I did have another great summer. Arriving with a large Mercury sedan helped to make a lot of friends. Occasionally, I would go on one of my long walks when I would get down, but most of the times on my day off I had a car full of counselors. Waterfront counselors had Wednesdays off. Day off meant exactly that, twenty-four hours of freedom. One time we left early and drove to the World's Exposition in Montreal. I had the thrill of riding in a hydrofoil. Another time we went to Fort Ticonderoga. On the grassy field in front of the fort, I experienced my first heavy petting session.

Of all the help that I received from Dr. Hauer, he really came through in spades during my last year at MSC. My senior year had the understandable stresses of high school student teaching, graduation recital, and finding a job. Still, I managed to give my senior recital in November, student teach at a high school in Newton which was about fifteen miles from Sparta, and live at home for four weeks without any major blow-ups.

In the spring, Charles, my brother, who is four years younger, had just heard that he had received a full-ride Navy ROTC scholarship to the University of Illinois. I was very excited for him and drove to Sparta on Saturday. Spending the whole weekend was still too chancy, and I wasn't looking for trouble. There was a real air of celebration. My mother favored my brother, but that was OK, because all attention was on him. I didn't think anything could go wrong.

We were having a very pleasant brunch on Sunday morning. (My dad was now stationed in Long Island.) My mother casually asked me what my plans were after graduation. I told her that nothing was definite, but that I might try to teach near Montclair and live with a few music major friends. She went violent.

"You mean that while your brother is in Champaign, and your father is in Long Island, that I am going to rot here alone in Sparta?"

My brother interjected (unfortunately with comic inflection), "Why don't you sell the house and move to Long Island." She took the large glass juice pitcher and threw it at me. I had to duck, and it barely missed hitting me. It crashed against the wall and splashed me with orange juice. My brother looked at me and said, "Get out of here, now!"

I jumped up, grabbed my purse and keys, and ran to my car. All the while she was yelling, "You come back here, you SOB, you come back here." I left everything, piano music, raincoat, suitcase. It was raining hard, and I got soaked before I got in the car. I was sobbing. In order to drive east from Sparta in the direction of Montclair, one had to go down Mase Mountain, which was not easy to navigate even in good weather. I really don't know how I made it down the mountain (maybe a guardian angel was with me.)

I drove to Dr. Hauer's house. (I had also visited his house previously, but honestly never thought I would really end up there. Driving to his house in Rockaway was just a way of occasionally recharging my emotional batteries.) When I arrived at his house, I was a mess. I was wet from the rain, sticky from the orange juice, and crying. He answered the door, and I blurted out, "She tried to kill me in front of my brother; she tried to kill me!"

She had crossed another line. Usually she lashed out at me when no one was around, or she would ask my brother to leave the house before punishing me. This time she tried to assault me in front of him. Her war with me was no longer private.

Dr. Hauer told me he was with a client but would speak with me afterwards. When I finally got to talk with him, I remember his concerns were more global. He was concerned about what had happened to me, but he was also concerned about my brother. "Do you think your brother is safe? Should I call the police?" I told him that she would never do anything to him. (Years later I learned that my brother had to physically restrain my mother from getting in her car and going after me.)

I told him that as much as I wanted to get to his house, I also had feelings that driving off Mase Mountain wasn't a bad idea either. He asked me point blank if I was suicidal. This was the first time I had been directly confronted with that question. Although crashing through a rail off Mase Mountain had occurred to me, I told him, "No." I had a choir concert the next day, and I was one of the stronger altos, and I thought I was feeling a little better. He offered to drive me back to Montclair. I said that wasn't a good idea, because I would have to leave my car, and how would I get it. I spent a few hours in his home and finally felt that I could drive back safely.

I shudder to think what might have happened if I had not stopped at Dr. Hauer's house. The weather was lousy. The trip involved traveling on US Route 46, which was known as a "skull and crossbones" highway. The divided highway was old, had narrow lanes, minimal shoulder, and a cement divider. Cars were always crashing. MSC lost a few students each year to US Route 46.

When I got back, Diane, my roommate, said that my mother had been calling every half hour, and I had better call her and tell her I had arrived safely. I told her I never wanted to speak to my mother again and to tell Mother that I was asleep the next time she called. The calls temporarily stopped. About two in the morning the phone rang, and I picked it up. My mother was audibly crying. She didn't apologize. All I heard was, "I was so worried." I dropped the receiver on the phone without speaking. I sang in the concert on Monday. I really don't know how I did it. One of my alto friends had to guide me off the risers. Looking back, I think I was in shock.

I saw Dr. Hauer that week, and I started the conversation with, "Well, I don't think I can teach in this area." He responded with, "I don't think you should teach anywhere in New Jersey." We both laughed. He suggested a few alternative plans but warned me that there might be a lag time before being able to leave home. I opted to join the US Navy; they had a timetable.

I saw him only a few more times. Then it was exams, graduation, and my undergraduate days were over. A year later while in the Navy, I hitched a military ride to attend a good friend's senior piano recital. I was hoping to stop and see Dr. Hauer while at Montclair. Unfortunately, the Kent State massacre closed the campus, and I was not able to see him.

I've had other guardian angels in the form of therapists, but Dr. Hauer was my first therapist, and like a first love, he will always remain special. Simply put, he not only got me through college, he opened the door to a better me---a guardian angel.

Rowena Staniseski Rotolo,

College Dorm mate,
Montclair State College (1965-1969)

1964. Eighteen years old. Lovely Rowena. I first met Rowena when I was a freshman living on the seventh floor of the Freeman Hall dormitory at MSC. She was a sophomore, and I admired her. She seemed like the perfect student. She was friendly, intelligent, and always dressed well. She put on make-up before breakfast and always wore rollers at night, so she would have the perfect hair flip the next morning. She was a French major and did well in her classes.

However, the confident appearance and demeanor belied a life that hadn't been kind to Rowena. I would later learn that she also was allowed to live in the dorm as a psychological hardship case. Rowena's parents had divorced, and her mother was an alcoholic. Rowena had a younger sister that was living at home and was always in some sort of trouble. Rowena said that her sister had never really adjusted to the divorce, blamed her alcoholic mother, and acted out continually. There was frequent fighting between her sister and mother making living at home intolerable for Rowena.

Rowena asked me if I had a nickname because Cynthia was just too long. I told her I didn't have one, and the common shortened version, Cindy, was not for me—since I didn't think I was the bubbly cheerleader type. She said, "How about Cy (pronounced "sigh")?" I was flattered that she would take the time to give me an unusual nickname. Soon everybody on the seventh floor was calling me Cy.

The first time I went home, my mother asked me how I was getting along with my dorm mates. I told her, "Very well, and I've been given a nickname, Cy." My mother said, "Cy? That's a man's name, like Cyrus McCormick." She continued by saying that it wasn't that they liked me, but instead they were making fun of me. I thought about it for a while and wondered if it was true. When I got back to the dorm, I asked Rowena if she knew the name Cy was a nickname for Cyrus. She said she really hadn't thought about it. She selected the first two letters of my name much like her nickname, "Ro."

My mother was adamant that I call home once a week. Every Wednesday at seven thirty in the evening, I would go to the pay phone on the floor and make a collect call. Sometimes the calls were pleasant, and other times they were obnoxious. She would ask me questions: What was I eating, was I doing my laundry, how much sleep was I getting, how were my menstrual periods, and was I regular? She never asked me about my classes or music studies. I lied a lot to keep her satisfied. I resented making those calls and started to call late. She of course would be angry and tell me that since they were paying for my college education, I should at least be punctual when I called.

Sometimes I would just hold out the receiver and let a few dorm mates listen to her diatribe. But having her yell about being late was better than answering all those invasive questions. I talked to Ro about not wanting to call. She told me that I didn't have to call every week. After all, what was my mother going to do? She surely was not going to drive to Montclair and chastise me. I took her advice and didn't call the next week. I called the following week, and my mother let me know what an ungrateful person I was. I interjected that if she kept on railing at me, I wouldn't call her the following week. I finally had the upper hand.

MSC did not have national fraternities or sororities, but we did have local Greek clubs. Bids were handed out in the spring. Only a few girls received bids in the freshman year. More bids were handed out to sophomores, and I was invited to join two sororities.

My suitemates, Ro and Joyce S. were members of Lambda Omega Tau. Occasionally some of the other members would come to their dorm room, and they seemed like a friendly group. They told me that they would welcome a music major since one of the campus activities was the Greek a cappella sing, and I was flattered. I also received a bid to Mu Sigma, and when I met their sisters, I knew this group was more to my liking. But I didn't want to hurt Ro and Joyce's feeling by not choosing their club. I decided that I wouldn't upset anyone and told Ro that I wasn't joining any sorority.

Rowena had one vice; she smoked heavily. But if Rowena walked into your room with a cigarette and an ashtray, you knew that you were going to get at least ten minutes of her quality time. She asked me which sorority I liked better, and I dodged the question by saying both groups had nice members. She was persistent and asked me, "Which one would you rather join?" I told her, "Mu Sigma. Are you angry that I'm not joining Lambda Omega Tau?" She told me that I should join the group that I wanted even if it wasn't hers. She said, "I want you to be happy with your choice; you're really a nice person and you deserve that." I joined Mu Sigma.

Although I moved off campus in my junior year, I still kept in contact with Ro. Many times we would meet in the Freeman Hall cafeteria for lunch. During one of those lunches she showed me her engagement ring and asked if I would stand up to her wedding. I was so touched by that invitation. Her wedding was planned for July, and I told her that I wasn't going anywhere that summer and would be able to be one of her bridesmaids. As it turned out, I had to amend my summer plans (due to another "mother mortar") and worked as a waterfront instructor at Camp Dunmore in Vermont. Shortly after I arrived at the camp, I asked the directors if I could have Friday and Saturday off for the wedding. They said I could have from midnight Thursday to noon on Sunday when the campers' parents came to visit.

I started driving at two in the morning on Friday to get to New Jersey for the fitting of my dress, and I left at four in the morning on Sunday morning to make it back to camp to greet the parents. I was fairly exhausted for the next few days, but it had been worth it to stand up for Ro.

The last time I saw Rowena was during my first year in the Navy when I hitched a military ride to the east coast. The first thing she said was, "Please wear your uniform; I want to see you in it." When I visited her, she told me I looked great and was really proud of me that I had survived basic training and was enjoying being a naval officer. She also told me that she was pregnant, and I told her how happy I was for her.

Rowena was friendly to everyone, but I felt especially warmed by her kindness to me. Unfortunately, she died much too young. She was a guardian angel.

Diane T.,

Off campus Roommate, Montclair State College (1964-1968)

1964. Seventeen years old. I met Diane my freshman year. We both played French horn in the marching band. She was a Spanish major but spent a lot of time in the music building. She also joined Sigma Alpha Iota, the professional women's music fraternity, the same year I did.

After my sophomore year, I was looking for something a little more independent than dorm life. Diane also said she was tired of the eleven o'clock popcorn parties and the general noise level. We decided to room together. My mother was totally against the idea. At this time, Mother knew nothing about my therapy, but I did have a car and told her that by living off campus I could play in community orchestras and not have to worry about the eleven o'clock dorm curfew. She said she would allow it only if I bought a three-meal ticket at Freeman Hall. The compromise was OK with me.

We were a good pair. I learned a lot about Don Quixote from her, she got some theory and music history tidbits from me, and I taught her how to drive. She knew I was seeing Dr. Hauer, but she wasn't overly sympathetic. In fact, many times she kicked my ass. Most of the times I saw Dr. Hauer during the school day. That was good, since if I had a bad session, I could resurface by the end of the day. Sometimes Dr. Hauer was very busy, and he could only see me in the late afternoon. I would go directly back to the house after a session. Periodically, I came home obnoxiously depressed. "God, I am so depressed. I wish I could jump in the Pacific Ocean."

To which she replied, "How about the Hudson River?"

I said that I wasn't that depressed. We both laughed and went out for dinner. "The Hudson River" became our private joke.

Diane had been raised Catholic and was trying to assert her independence with respect to attending mass every Sunday. We lived about three miles from the Clifton parish, which had masses every Sunday from six in the morning to five in the afternoon. She would tell me, "I'm going to get up early, take your car, go to mass and get it over with, and jump back in bed." Of course six would come and go, and she was still in bed. She then said that she would make the seven thirty mass. She'd miss that one and a few others. Finally, she and I would run into church just before the bell rang for the five o'clock mass. After mass, I would say, "Diane, are we going through this again next Sunday?"

Whenever Diane would date someone more than a few times, she would start to knit him a long-sleeved sweater. Then it seemed the relationship would break off just as she was finishing the sweater. This happened a couple of times. As she was working on another sweater, I walked into her room and said, "Look's like Ed has only a few more dates with you." She looked at me quizzically. "Diane, don't you realize that you've never given those sweaters away? Always trust a crazy."

If my mother called, she could be polite, but she could also lie like a rogue if I didn't want to talk to her. And when another round of mother-mortars flew in from Sparta, she was there for me. Her favorite expression was, "Is this a Hudson thing, do I need to pack for San Francisco, or do you need to talk to Dr. Hauer?"

One Sunday after mass we stopped at West's Diner. We barely had enough for the bill and were in a quandary as to whether or not to leave what little we had for a tip. We chose to leave the eleven cents. As we were walking to the car, the waitress came out and threw the coins at us, yelling, "Girls, don't forget your car fare!" It made Diane angry; I just melted and started crying.

Monday was a monthly SAI meeting, and I didn't know it, but she had told our fraternity sisters about the incident. We went to West's Diner, and lo and behold, were served by the same waitress. When it was time to tip the waitress, my friends at the table smiled at me, and they each pulled out a penny and a dime. I told Dr. Hauer about the incident, and he commented that it was rather cruel, but that I had some good friends.

On a sunny Sunday in the fall of our senior year, we decided to ditch our studies and go apple picking. We rationalized that we would be able to practice our people skills. We enjoyed beautiful weather and met some other college students who were also taking a break. After a refreshing day away, we threw our bag of apples in the back of the car and headed home through the hilly country of northwest New Jersey. I was driving, and all of sudden I couldn't go any faster than twenty miles per hour. I tried pressing the accelerator harder but could go no faster. I was very concerned that someone traveling at the normal speed might not see us and ram into us, and I pulled off the road.

We stepped out of the car, put the hood up, and soon a man stopped to assist us. We told him our problem, and of course he first asked us if we were out of gas. Then he sat down in the driver's seat to find out what was wrong. In about two minutes he came out of the car and said, "Here's your problem." He was holding a small apple. He told us that it was wedged between the accelerator and the floor board. We were initially embarrassed, but I was relieved that we wouldn't have to abandon the car. Then he said, "You girls, you're college students, right?" And we jumped in, "Yes, we're at Montclair; we're going to be teachers." The look on his face was priceless. It read, "Oh my God, I hope you don't teach in my kids' district." We laughed about that all the way back to Montclair.

She knew I had to leave the area after college, but she thought that joining the Navy was self-flagellating. "Aren't you tired of following orders?" After I was commissioned, I wrote to her that I had made it. Half of our class ran away, begged to get out, or washed out, but I stuck it out. She wrote back and responded with, "Glad you didn't jump in the Hudson!"

Diane was a good friend, a great roommate, and someone who could not only make me laugh, but laugh at myself-- a guardian angel.

Interlude 1

United States Navy,
(1968-1970)

1968. Twenty-one years old. I graduated from Montclair State College on Wednesday, June fifth. I was to report to the naval base at Newport, Rhode Island, on Sunday, June twenty-third, which meant I had about three weeks off. I arranged to spend a week in Florida with my close college friend, Martha M., and we stayed with my grandparents. Therefore, I only had a few weeks to manage relations with my mother before reporting to the Women Officers' School in Newport. As I remember, things were pretty uneventful and somewhat pleasant.

I drove up to Newport in my Mercury. I clearly remember the exhilaration. "I am truly on my own. I am free." The '60 Merc was a solid car, and I drove about seventy miles per hour all the way. About an hour before reaching the base, I had a right front tire blowout. I pulled off the road and wondered what to do. A retired chief petty officer (USN) stopped and changed the tire—a guardian angel? I made it to the base with time to spare.

Military training is an amazing operation. We were shown our quarters and introduced to our military directors. We were measured for uniforms, underwent a physical, and given vaccinations with a gun-type mechanism. We were taught to drill, spit-shine our shoes, starch and iron our uniforms.

We were taught how to make a military bed with mitered corners. (They measured the angles with a protractor.)

We also attended academic classes: Introduction to the Navy, Naval Operations, Naval Justice, and Naval History. We stood inspection at 7:00 a.m. and were "gigged" for the slightest infraction (collar with wrinkle = 1 gig; 5 gigs = 1 demerit). Each week our grades were posted. I kept a high academic rank, but my military rank was much lower. I gave it my best shot, but if my shoes didn't look like mirrors, I didn't get upset. We started out with a class close to one hundred women. At the end of the eight weeks—half were gone.

I asked my dad to commission me, and the whole family was there on August 23, 1968 to witness me take the oath. It was rather special.

The next eight weeks we were indoctrinated as officers. We still had to stand inspection, and keep our rooms spotless, but other rules were more relaxed. We used to joke that the last eight weeks was to see if we could keep our mouth shut and hold our liquor. I had asked for orders to Hawaii or Washington, DC. I was a little disappointed but still excited about my first billet: Educational Service Officer, Naval Administrative Command, Great Lakes Naval Base, Illinois.

I drove back to Sparta in October and had a week's leave to get ready for the trip to Great Lakes Naval Base. There were no major blowups, but there almost was one. I have always had a "thing" about shoes—not the Imelda Marcos thing of collecting a hundred pairs—but shoes that I have worn mean something to me. I had a pair of Bass loafers that lasted my four years at Montclair. These were the shoes in which I walked to class, practiced, studied, walked to Dr. Edward's house, saw Dr. Hauer, went to Pt. Pleasant, went to Greenwich Village, and went to two different summer camps. They held me! And, I was looking forward to wearing them as a naval officer. I was collecting my stuff for the trip to Great Lakes and noticed that they weren't in my closet. I asked my mother if she had seen them. She said she tossed them out since they were a little shabby. She had once again gone through my things without regard for me. Inwardly I was very sad and upset, and then I just shrugged it off.

I expected to throw all my stuff in the old Merc and head west by myself. My mother said that she would like to drive with me, because she thought it would be safer. I told her that I had driven to Vermont and Rhode Island alone, I had driven all over New Jersey, I had driven in New York City and

Interlude 1

Long Island; I could handle the drive to Chicago. She was insistent and also said that it would be an opportunity to visit Charles, my brother, at the University of Illinois. I thought that was ludicrous since he was a freshman and had just arrived there. We got close to a fight, but I surrendered. ("In one week I will be far away from you. Just keep your mouth closed.")

My date to report was October 29, 1968. We started out on October 26. On the second day, the heater in the Mercury went out.

The weather was fair, and we were driving essentially west so the sun's radiant energy kept the car warm. We arrived at the University of Illinois in Urbana on October 27 and had dinner with Charles at his dorm, Bromley Hall.

The weather changed dramatically, and we knew the heater would have to be repaired. We pulled into the service bay area of a Ford dealer, and my mother said, "Why don't you flirt with the mechanic, and then maybe they'll fix it quickly?" That about did it. I told her to wait in the car, and I would see how much time it would take for them to assess the problem. She came into the service waiting area anyway. I was thinking to myself. "Flirt with the mechanic? You, who never encouraged my femininity, who told me that when I wore lipstick it looked like a monkey's ass, you want me sashay in and give someone the batty eye?"

With sixteen weeks of military training, I walked up to the service desk and said, "Good morning, I am Ensign Cynthia Kanapicki, and I have a slight problem. I am traveling with my mother to Great Lakes, and we have a faulty heater. I have to report in by this afternoon." (This was a lie; my report date was the next day.) "Is there a mechanic that might be able to assist us?" I looked at my mother; she was floored. The dealership had us on our way in about an hour. (While at officer candidate school, we were told that it is verboten for an officer to pull rank on a civilian citizen except in times of national emergency. Well, I guess I pulled rank on the clerk and my mother, and we were not under fire.)

We checked in at the Waukegan Holiday Inn and went to the dining room. When the waiter came, I asked if there were any birthday drink specials, since today, October 28, was my twenty-second birthday. My mother had forgotten. She was extremely apologetic saying that the trip and the faulty heater had made her lose track of the days.

The next time I saw my parents was over the July Fourth weekend in 1969. I didn't tell them I was coming. I wore my uniform, flew standby to Kennedy, and took the bus to New Jersey. They greeted me warmly. We went upstairs for a meal, and I sat there with my hands on the table. My father was the first to notice the engagement ring. I had not told them about Lt. Joe G. I showed them pictures of us in uniform and also in casual clothes. My mother asked if we had set a date, and I told her, yes, December 31, in Winston-Salem, North Carolina. I told her that Joe's brother was a minister, and Joe wanted him to perform the ceremony. My dad started tearing; he was so happy for me. My mother piped up, "Don't you think that you should complete your first tour of duty before thinking about marrying?" (Well, one out of two isn't bad.)

One morning a nurse from the BOQ was taken by ambulance to the hospital; she had botched a self-abortion. Joe and I had been having sexual relations, and I thought that birth control pills might be a wise idea. A few weeks after I was taking the contraceptives, I started to feel blue. I knew the signs of depression, but I attributed it to the oncoming of fall.

I had a ball flying almost every other weekend to Norfolk to see Joe during the summer. We had fun in the sun. (I lost my virginity on the beach at Virginia Beach, which I still think is somewhat funny.) My weather blues persisted. Unfortunately, I'll never really know if it was the birth control pills or just that I was prone to depression, but I'd bet that the contraceptives played a role. Joe and I would communicate by the Watts government phone line. He was getting excited about the wedding and my moving to Norfolk, and I was becoming listless and disinterested. I tried to brighten up but couldn't. On December 21, I called off the wedding.

I called my parents to give them the news, and my mother answered the phone. She asked me if I might reconsider. I told her no. She wanted to know what she should do with all the gifts. I told her I would assume the cost of returning the gifts. During a later call, she said she didn't want to talk with me anymore. I thought that she was referring to discussing the called-off wedding. She said, no, that she was not talking to me at all. And she didn't.

In the spring of 1970, my parents drove up to see Charles and me. I was very anxious about her coming. When they arrived, I was working on a project and told them I would meet them at the BOQ for lunch. My parents were already at the BOQ and chatting with some of the officers. I joined in the conversation. Then we went down to lunch, and my mother had everybody laughing at all her Navy stories. My mother needed to use the restroom, and I said, "Why don't you just come up to my room?"

Interlude 1

While we were both in the bathroom, I told her that I really enjoyed seeing her, and that I was so sorry about the canceled wedding, but I was happy that she was talking to me. I'll never forget what she did.

She was facing me and then she turned away. Then she turned back to face me with a totally different, icy glare. She turned away again as if to say, "I was talking to them, not to you."

The eight-month moratorium on our communication ended in October of 1970 (three months after my separation from the Navy). My parents had flown to Chicago for my paternal grandmother's funeral, and she couldn't avoid speaking to me since they were staying in my apartment.

My first year, I was the Educational Services Officer. During my second year, I became the Assistant Project Transition Officer. This was a Department of Defense program initiated to keep separated service men, especially those who fought in Vietnam, from going on welfare. I worked jointly with the hospital side looking for training opportunities for servicemen leaving the Navy.

Upon reflection I was a pretty good officer. My job as Educational Services Officer was mostly supervisory and administrative, which meant that if things were going well, it was sort of boring. The real excitement only came when there were problems.

I made one major mistake, and it reflected on my annual fitness report. As Educational Services Officer, I oversaw the rating exams that were given yearly. The rating exams were proficiency exams that would, in part, allow enlisted personnel to advance to the next pay grade. Of course, I had a manual to follow and previous records from the former ESO, but I had to set it up myself. In addition to the basics of reserving the testing location, drafting proctors, and dissemination of information (publicity), I had to log in all the exams and keep accurate records.

Some of the exams contained questions with confidential material. I received a temporary Secret clearance to handle most of the exams, but some ratings, like Electronic Technician, required a Top Secret clearance, and I needed to follow a different protocol. In addition to all that, I had to take care of hospitality, coffee and sweet rolls for the proctors.

There was one final problem. The SS (Ship's Steward) exam was frequently compromised. Mostly Filipino men filled the SS rating at that time. These were the sailors that were cooks and stewards on ships and staffed the BOQ. The ship's stewards would take the exams, there would be evidence of collusion, and the results would be nullified. I received a directive from Washington, DC, which stated that at no time could the SS exams be out of my custody—nor was I to open the package and examine the contents. The exams could be left in my safe if I was the only one with the combination.

On the day of the exams, I picked up the exams from the safe and headed over to the testing center on the other side of the base. In nervous anticipation of the day's events, nature called, and I chose to stop at the BOQ to use the ground floor restroom. The SS exams were now in my locked trunk. I came back to my car and drove to the test center.

I had planned well, and there were no complaints, plenty of proctors, and plenty of coffee. The top-secret exams were handled properly, and all the other exams were shipped to the Naval Testing Center. I had to file a custody report on the SS Exams. I briefly had to write where the exams were from the time they were delivered until the test booklets were opened. On an hourly time sheet I wrote SAFE, PERSONAL CUSTODY, LOCKED AUTOMOBILE TRUNK, PERSONAL CUSTODY, TESTING CENTER. I signed my name and rank and sent it in with the exams.

A few days later, my immediate boss called me in. He told me that I had made a serious mistake leaving the exams in my trunk when I wasn't in the car. There was no way to prove that the exams had not been compromised. I, of course, countered that the box was sealed, the inner package was unopened, and that I felt sure that nothing had happened.

But he was right, there was broken custody. I later had a dressing down by the executive officer and had to endure a hashing out of my mistake. I called my dad and asked him what he would have done. He said that under the circumstances he would have taken the exams with him while using the restroom. I said, "You mean you would have taken the package into the stall?" He said that he would have. (I find it terribly ironic that my one major mistake in the US Navy was because I took a crap. [*vide infra*]

As it turned out, the SS Exams were compromised even before I went to the bathroom. A sympathetic officer on a ship in the Pacific shared some of the information from the test booklet with his stewards.

Overall the Navy was a great experience. When I first arrived, I enjoyed being teased about being an ensign (the lowest officer's rank in the Navy). I was usually referred to as "the ensign."

"Good morning, Ensign. How goes the Navy?"

Interlude 1

I met some very interesting people. Dinner conversations were scintillating. I didn't have much worldly experience, but I could talk music. If some officer was thinking about choosing an opera to see at the Lyric Opera in Chicago, I could at least differentiate the tragedies from the comedies.

I enjoyed being the "different one." There were many nurses living in the BOQ, but there were few line officers. I was frequently asked, "Since you're not a nurse, why are you in the Navy?" My favorite response was, "Money, sex, and power—and not necessarily in that order." Once I hitched a military ride to Andrews Air Force Base. I was, of course, in uniform. I took transportation to the officers' club to have dinner and to find out how to get to Washington National so I could fly to LaGuardia. When I walked into the Air Force officers' club at Andrews, a few officers chimed, "Well, here comes the Navy." I enjoyed those moments.

I dated occasionally but didn't "put out." The scuttlebutt was that I was the virgin ensign. That did not bother me at all. Occasionally, a group of us would go to a local bar, and I would often drive because I had the big Merc. On one occasion, I drank too much to drive back to the base, and I didn't trust anyone to drive the car. We all piled into a couple of taxis and left.

My boss called me on Monday morning. He asked, "Did I see your damn car at two o'clock in the morning in front of some damn bar in Waukegan?"

I replied, "That's affirmative, sir; however, at the time you saw it, I was back at the BOQ." Of the many things I learned in the service, one was how to answer a question. Say yes or no, validate the questioner's observation, then qualify your response. To which he replied,

"Smart move, Ensign, you'll make (Lt.) j.g."

Lt. Serena Y.

US Navy, Great Lakes Naval Base, Great Lakes, Illinois (1969-1970)

I lived in the BOQ during my two years at Great Lakes. Most of my roommates were either temporary, reservists for two weeks, or officers in transition awaiting discharge, e.g. nurses who got pregnant. The first line officer roommate I had was Lt. Serena Y. She had just come from Hawaii, and this was her third tour of duty. It was a welcome relief to meet someone who wasn't puking in my bathroom (reservists) or just waiting to get out of the Navy.

We hit it off immediately. Since she had a dog, she only stayed in the BOQ long enough to find an apartment. We frequently ate lunch together and occasionally celebrated payday steak night by going to different restaurants.

She continually told me that Great Lakes was not the real Navy. Most people were just marking time waiting for their next assignments to an operational base. This was true. Great Lakes Naval Base was the Recruit Training Center, the Service School command, and the Administrative Command that oversaw the other two. Frequently, when I approached my boss with an administrative issue, he would say, "I'm just a goddamn ship's navigator, how the hell should I know?" He was counting the days until his next sea-duty billet.

I have always had fine, limp hair. When I was younger, my mother would put pin curls in my hair and admonish me to take them out right before my school picture was taken. If I have any pleasant features, my hair is not one of them. The naval uniform fit me well, but the hat, which was heavy, matted down my hair. Apparently, my boss thought that it was unbecoming enough that he asked Serena to suggest I do something. (What an order!) She did, and though I was taken aback by the emphasis on my appearance as opposed to my competence, I followed through. I went to the best salon in Waukegan and explained my problem. His suggestion was to either dye my hair with my natural color or lighten it. Thus, I became a semi-blonde at the request of the United States Navy.

Serena and I would also spend time laughing at the nurses. (Now I know my list of guardian angels has an R.N. I surely don't want to rile anyone by saying that some of them were not smart, but some of them weren't.)

There was a large contingent of docs living at the BOQ. Many of them were unhappy campers. They had been drafted to serve and forced to leave their practices and families. But there also were a few unmarried docs, and the unattached nurses would fawn all over them. Serena and I would laugh at the inanity of their behavior and conversations. During one of our pay-day steak nights, I said, "I don't want to marry a doctor; I want to be one!" Serena said, "Why don't you?"

When I received my letter inviting me to augment into the regular Navy, I told her it was a difficult decision whether to stay in the Navy or try to get into medical school. So, we talked it about it and agreed that if I stayed in the Navy, I would never have a chance at medical school, but if I went to medical school, I could come back into the Navy. (What a friend.)

We were both dating occasionally, and we made a pact. She would stand up at my wedding, and I would stand up at hers. She later resigned her commission and married an Army officer. I flew down to Ft. Benning, Georgia, and was one of her bridesmaids.

Aftermath: I left the Navy in 1970 and got married two years later in August 1972. My father had retired from the Navy in 1969, and my parents were now living in Corpus Christi, Texas.

Michael and I discussed where we would get married. We were going to have a very small wedding, and most of the people invited were going to be from the groom's side. I knew it would anger my mother if I were to marry in a church in Highland Park where Michael lived. I suggested that we get married in the naval base chapel at Great Lakes, and Lance, Michael's cousin, could officiate.

Then came the discussion of the wedding plans in the spring of 1972. My parents had visited my brother in Champaign at the University of Illinois and stopped in Chicago to visit me. I said that I only would have one attendant, Serena, my matron of honor.

My parents looked at me and said, "Really?" I told them Serena and I had made a pact while we were both in the Navy, and I was following through. The reason why they were questioning me was because Serena is African-American. Serena had not only met my parents, she had graciously invited them to stay at her apartment the first time they visited me during the spring of 1969. My mother had told me that Serena was quite a gal. (My mother was never easily impressed.)

My mother even came up with the proverbial, "What will my friends think?" I told them it was my wedding, it was going to be small, about twenty-five people, and I wasn't asking for much. And then my dad, "Don't Rock the Boat Kaz," said, "Are you trying to make a political statement?" And you know what I did? I did nothing. I didn't stand up for Serena. I stormed out of the room saying, "Fine, whatever you want!"

To this day I am ashamed that I buckled. My Aunt Vickie was my matron of honor. Serena flew up to the wedding and attended the rehearsal dinner. My wedding was a happy day. It rained like hell, but it was a small and lovely affair.

Serena took me at face value. She didn't treat me like I was a psychological hardship case that had three years of therapy in college. We both were naval officers. We both had endured officer candidate training. We both had an assigned billet at Great Lakes, and we both enjoyed going to the officers' club after work on Friday and having a beer. In 1968 there were 6,000 male line officers in the Navy and 600 female line officers; we were part of an elite club.

Serena was the guardian angel that allowed me to look at myself as a fully functioning young adult.

Interlude 2
Chicago, Illinois (1978-1979)

1978. Thirty-two years old. My daughter, Anna, was born on April 15, 1978. Although it was a fairly normal pregnancy, during the last month routine tests indicated she might be underdeveloped according to her gestational age. I was asked if my dates might be wrong. I told the clinic that I knew the exact date that I conceived since my husband was at a summer music festival at Indiana University, and I only visited him once. She was also in a breech position. I was given a C-section, and Anna was born at 11:30 p.m. on Saturday. Except for a dent on her head, she appeared to be OK.

As it turned out, I had a bicornate uterus, which is normal for sheep but not for humans. Anna was squished into one side and the enzymes in the amniotic fluid were not circulating, generating misleading values. Anna was OK, but I was not.

By Sunday afternoon I had a fever, and on Monday it was determined that I had pneumonia, and I was moved off the maternity floor. My parents flew in on Monday and when my mother saw me, I was still pretty ill. Her first comment to me was, "Well, I can see you weren't fooling around." (Anna favored Michael.) On Thursday I was finally able to hold Anna. I tried to nurse her but was unsuccessful. On Friday I was discharged from the hospital.

When I got back to our apartment, I could tell things were very tense between Michael and my mother. Per her usual modus operandi, she was bossing everybody around. She even told Michael where to hang up his towel in the bathroom, which did not please him at all. She had bought formula since she didn't think I would be able to give Anna the nutrition she needed. The tenser I got, the less milk I gave, and the more my mother would force the issue of feeding Anna with formula. Michael was getting angry, and I was getting discouraged. Finally my parents left, but not before my mother demanded that I arrange to stay with my in-laws. Now my in-laws are wonderful people, but I just wanted to be alone with Anna. After a week's stay in Highland Park with my in-laws, I went home and just became a contented cow.

Michael had been trying to find a professional French horn position in an orchestra for a couple of years. His teacher recommended that he attend the Aspen Music Festival in Colorado which lasted eight weeks. Although I was on maternity leave, we knew we couldn't both go; we couldn't afford it. We would be paying double rent and couldn't do it. I really missed Michael and decided that we could pay double rent for one month.

Colorado was absolutely gorgeous, but I was not able to enjoy it. Weekends were filled with concerts so there was little family time. I put Anna in an infant back-pack carrier and took her for a walk. When I came back it looked like her skin had been ironed. (The sun's rays are more effective at higher altitudes.) Basically, I was stuck inside with an infant, the book *Shogun*, and double-vision television. However, through connections at Aspen, Michael was able to get a job playing first horn in an opera orchestra in Kassel, Germany.

Michael left for Kassel, Germany, shortly after we returned to Chicago. Although my maternity leave officially ended October 15, I found a sitter for Anna and went back to work in September. I felt hopeful for Michael, and it was good to be back in the lab. Of course having a new baby, most people were quite generous in occasionally letting me start late or leave early. I was productive in the lab and felt that I was handling things pretty well.

The Chicago winter of 1978–79 was especially brutal. Commuting from MRH to Rogers Park took a minimum of three hours. Similar to Japan, the Chicago Transit Authority (CTA) had people shovers, pushing people onto the trains. The intra-city elevated trains stopped before the

Interlude 2

end of the line, and we had to cram on buses. Because I got home so late, I had to hire a second sitter to relieve the first sitter. Still, I was doing OK, because I thought Michael was doing OK in Germany.

The music conductor of the State Opera Orchestra in Kassel, Germany was English. This caused some political strife within the orchestra, and as a result, Michael lost his position. He came home in February. He had some great playing experience and had performed many operas.

Michael now started to audition for orchestras in the United States. Michael always did well; he would call me up and tell me that he had made the first cut. There might be as many as twenty musicians competing for the position. The final audition was usually down to three or four. But the next call to me would be that he was home and would need a ride from the airport. He auditioned everywhere. When Michael was in Kassel, he was paid with Deutsch Marks and came home with a fine surplus. Now our money was going to the airlines, and we were eating into our savings. The finances weren't as deflating as the hopefulness followed by the letdown. It really started to drain me.

To add to the mix, Michael's brother, who like me had received his MS in biology at the Illinois Institute of Technology, was graduating from Loyola Medical School. My graduate friend from IIT, Karen M. S., had been accepted to medical school at the University of Illinois—and she was seven months pregnant. It felt like I had been hit in the head with a Chinese gong, "You were really never qualified to go to medical school."

My parents drove up to Chicago to help celebrate Anna's first birthday, which fell on Easter. My in-laws had invited everybody to their home for the double celebration. On Saturday, my Dad and Michael went on some errand. While they were gone, my mother in true fashion started a litany of everything that she thought was wrong: Michael didn't have a good job, our apartment was inadequate, we didn't even have a parking space, Anna was not in a healthy environment, and my job was too far from where we lived. But the real barbs came when she droned on about Anna deserving better. She never said I was a poor mother in so many words, but that was the message. I didn't say a word. I couldn't because if I had started to comment on her observations, it might have escalated into a shouting match. So I sat there silently.

She ended her sermon with, "And you know what, your kitchen is backwards. The dish drainer is on the wrong side of the sink." I told her that I was left-handed, and that's the way I liked it. She replied that, for the rest of the world, it was still backwards.

I remember thinking, "Let's see, I can file all her other complaints under inadequate, but where do I file this one, insanity or comedy?"

I had previously arranged for a sitter for Anna so we all could go to a movie that evening. I was nobly trying to avoid any opportunity for conversation; my mother had a fine track record of being insulting. I also didn't want my mother to be the martyr and stay home while the three of us, Michael, Dad, and I, went out. But she wouldn't even consider that; she said she wanted to stay home with Anna. (Even as I write this, I realize that I was always hopeful for a change in her behavior. I thought that maybe she would enjoy babysitting my daughter, her granddaughter, and just relax a little.) We were going to a late movie, so Anna was near her bedtime before we left.

When we came back, Anna wakened and started crying, and I went to hold her. "Mother, I think she heard my voice, I'll get her." My mother said, "I'll take care of it. I know exactly what this child needs." and she refused to let me take her. I left and listened to Anna cry for what seemed like an eternity (probably ten minutes). I was angry and wanted to throw everyone out. Michael was furious and said, "Do something!" I couldn't. I knew the birthday celebration was at my in-laws the next day, and I didn't want to start anything that might end horribly. The next day my mother was her charming self in Highland Park. It made her behavior the night before seem only directed to me.

As a research lab tech there were many weekends that I had to check on a column that might be running or do the preliminary step of an experiment that would start on Monday. It wasn't unusual for me to go to the lab. But I also used the lab as a real escape hatch. The research floors were basically empty, and I could go into the lab and be totally by myself.

The next weekend I went to the lab and just started to think of all the things that were stressing me. I thought about my brother-in-law's graduation and Karen's acceptance into medical school. I thought about Michael's inability to land an orchestra position, and I thought about how my mother once again had told me that I was inadequate. And then, as it has happened in the past, I sort of lost track of the time. I had come to the lab in the early afternoon on Sunday. When I sat down at my bench it was one o'clock. The next thing I knew it was six, the sun was setting, and I had not moved from the bench. I grabbed my stuff and went home. Michael was a little upset that I was so late. I told him that it was really lucky that I had checked on my columns, because one of them had a crack, and I had to repack it before adding the antigen the next day. I lied.

But I knew I was in trouble.

My research assay had a two-hour antibody incubation time, which allowed me to do other things including going to the hospital library. I looked up the literature on depression. I took several self-inventory questionnaires: I was moderately depressed.

Dr. S., M.D.

Psychiatrist, Michael Reese Hospital
Chicago, Illinois (1979-1987)

1979. Thirty-one years old. I knew I needed some help, but I wasn't sure what to do next. I surely didn't want to ask anybody in pediatrics, my department. I also knew that social workers, psychologists, and psychiatrists practiced psychotherapy. So I let fate make my choice. I called up the Wexler outpatient clinic of MRH and said that I was not in major distress but needed to talk to someone. I asked them to give me a name of a social worker, psychiatrist, and psychologist that might have the time. By the end of the afternoon I had the name of three therapists. I decided to call them the next day around ten in the morning. Dr. S. called me back first and won the lottery.

When Dr. S. called back, I told him that I was a research technician who needed a little help. I told him that I didn't think it was serious. The analogy I used was the camera was in working order; I just needed to adjust the lens. My first appointment was May 1, 1979.

When I walked into his room, I was startled that he was younger than me: "Just how old are you?"

He told me, "twenty-nine," and asked if it made any difference. He said that if I would feel more comfortable with an older therapist, he would refer me to one. I told him, no, since fate got me here, I would stay. "It's just that I'm a bitter med school reject, and I competed for your class." And that's the way things started.

I told him that not being accepted into medical school was sort of taking over my life. I had been in therapy during college and found it helpful. I went on to say that I had a good marriage, a healthy kid, and a great job. I just needed to keep things in perspective, but I found it difficult. Dr. S. said he would see me the next week.

There must be a placebo effect of signing on for therapy, of taking that first step, and saying, "OK, I need help," because I felt like a million bucks walking out of his office. And another surprise was waiting for me.

The Group B-beta Streptococcus ELISA project that I had been working on for two years was accepted for presentation at an international conference in Boston the first week of October. The paper was going to be presented on the main stage, the hotel's grand ballroom. I offered my congratulations to Dr. G. and told him I wanted to go to Boston. He told me that there was no money in the grant to send a tech to Boston. I told him I would pay my own way and take vacation days to go. I told him, "You may be performing the concerto, but I wrote the music."

At the next visit to Dr. S. I almost bounced into his office. I told him things were going well. I was excited about the ELISA project being presented in Boston. Well, he handed me my healthy walking papers. He told me that he didn't think that I was in distress, and if I were to contact him, he would probably refer me to someone else. On the surface, it sounded good. I thanked him for his counsel and time and left. As soon as I closed the door behind me, I felt somewhat cut off and rejected. How could telling him that things were going well, which they honestly were, make me feel worse?

Michael went on another audition and came home empty-handed. I was outwardly sympathetic, but inwardly I just wanted all the auditions to stop. In a desperate attempt to shed the depression, I invited Michael's family over for a Mothers' Day brunch. The planning of the event only made me feel worse.

My brother-in-law's medical school graduation was in a few weeks, and everybody was excited about it. I knew that it would be the prime topic of conversation at the brunch. I knew I couldn't be there. It would be like miring myself in failure. On Mothers' Day, I got up early, took care of Anna, set the table, made the fruit salad, and left the house. I did not tell Michael where I was going or even that I was leaving. I of course went back to my lab and stared at the wall. And, in listing my stresses, I now had one more to add to the list. I felt rejected by Dr. S.

I came back in the early evening when I was sure everyone had left, and Michael was angry. "If you didn't want to attend the brunch, why the hell did you invite everybody over?" I told him I was trying to fight depression, and I was losing.

Two weeks later, my in-laws invited me to their house for Memorial Day. I declined; I was embarrassed at what I had done on Mother's Day. They suggested that we could meet at a park in Evanston and spend the day together. The weather on Memorial Day was lovely, warm and breezy. I sat around looking at everybody enjoying the day and wondered why I could see it but not feel it. I looked at Anna, lying on a blanket. I knew I didn't want to be her mother; I wanted to be like her—an infant.

I added everything up and decided that I wanted out. It was just a matter of planning how and when. I decided that I would drink a liter of barbital buffer. I would just go to sleep; there would be no pain. I took a couple of vials of barbital buffer salts and put them in my lab coat pocket. I had the method, and then I thought about the time. My brother-in-law was graduating early in June. I surely didn't want to ruin his graduation. My parent's anniversary was June 9; I had graduated on June 5; and one of my favorite composers, Schumann, was born June 8. It was too hard to choose a date, so I just put it off.

Someone needed to pick up a serum sample from a Northwestern clinic, and I volunteered to go. I didn't mind that my day might be disrupted. The travel on the MRH shuttle and the buses would give me plenty of time to just be depressed without having to hide it. I picked up the sample and then, instead of taking a bus to 30 North Michigan to wait for the hospital shuttle, I decided to walk the distance. When I started to cross over the Chicago River, I really had a strong impulse to jump. Here I had been thinking about a passive way of dying, and my mind was ready to have me jump into the river. I was frightened that I was really losing control. I felt that maybe by thinking and planning about suicide that I had made some sort of Faustian pact.

I went home after work and debated whether I should call Dr. S. I thought about it for at least three hours, getting close to the phone but not dialing. Finally, I called his answering service. I told him that I was not doing well at all. He said he could see me the next day at MRH.

I don't remember exactly what I said, but I did talk about the Chicago River.

He said, "Allow me to hospitalize you." Hearing how Gothic that sounded, with visions of *One Flew over the Cuckoo's Nest* dancing in my head, I replied, "How would that help?" He told me that he could see me every day and start me on some medication. I asked him about Michael, and he said he would contact him. I asked him, "What about work?" I function well." He said that this was more important than work. I tentatively agreed. I was to go to Barclay, a small psychiatric hospital on the north side.

I went back to my lab in sort of a cloud. In May he had given me my healthy walking papers; now I was going to a psychiatric hospital. But there was an inner part of me that knew I needed to be taken, at least temporarily, out of circulation.

Now, I had to tell my boss, Dr. G. I walked into his plush office and told him that I appreciated him seeing me on short notice. I told him that I had been seeing a psychiatrist for depression, and he suggested hospitalization. Dr. G. said that I should go. I said, "But I function and function well." Dr. G. said, "But you're paying a high price." I couldn't get over his generous support.

Aftermath: My five hospitalizations occurred during the thirteen years I worked at MRH for Dr. G. in the department of pediatrics. Work has always been a source of positive self-esteem for me. I was first author on a short methods paper, and I contributed to several others. I trained technicians, resident fellows, and developed an ELISA assay, but the important thing was that he always welcomed me back, and I never had to worry about losing my position.

I took the CTA bus to Barclay after work. Dr.S. stopped by later that evening. He told me, "Your health papers are officially rescinded." He thought I'd be there about ten days, and that I would start medication. Listening to him, the plan sounded so clinical—like "take a test tube, add the reagents, incubate, and read the results." But, I wasn't insulted, more intrigued. I told him that I would do my best to follow through with the plan. Then I took the vial of lethal barbital buffer salts out of my purse and said, "I'll let you keep this; but if this plan doesn't work, I want it back."

My roommate was an older woman who was being treated with electroconvulsive therapy. During my session, I asked Dr. S. about the method. It seemed so bizarre, straight out of a 1930's movie. He spent several minutes telling me the history of shock therapy. I appreciated that he talked to me as a teacher and not necessarily as a doctor or shrink who just listens and says nothing.

From my perspective, I felt a bond growing between us.

On Monday I was taken off suicidal precautions and allowed to go to the activities room. When I walked in, I immediately spotted the piano in the corner. It was a clunker, but it still had eighty-eight keys and a pedal. I asked if playing might disturb anyone, and they told me that this was the administration floor. I sat down and played lightly. As I warmed up, people started to drift in the room. Some just listened; others asked who I was. "Just a patient."

The first day I didn't play long. It felt so good to receive compliments. I was, of course, still having daily sessions with Dr. S. and had started an antidepressant, but I was feeling so good that I asked Michael to bring my art poster of Breton's "The Song of the Lark."

In retrospect, I probably should not have been allowed to play the piano. An affectionate public can mask a lot of issues. However, if I was forbidden to play the piano, I might have interpreted it as punitive. The piano does get in the way.

I took a battery of psychological tests on Thursday, and the research techs from my lab got permission to take me out to lunch on Friday. I was doing much better and was discharged on Sunday. I told Dr. S. that when I discussed the suicidal feelings with the nurse who was doing the discharge interview, the idea of suicide no longer seemed compatible with my feelings. He told me that the thought of suicide was now ego-dystonic.

There was no problem resuming work. People said, "Hey, I didn't see you around last week, were you on vacation?" I started to see Dr. S. weekly. I don't remember the topics I talked about, but I knew I was careful in how I said things. I monitored every word. I still was in the mode of trying to impress him that I was pretty sharp. Many times we parried words.

One exchange:

I said, "That's a point for your side."

He said, "I'm on the same side of the net."

I said, "Don't you believe that for a minute."

Still we made some progress. We talked about how my trying to get into medical school multiple times was an effort to get approval from my mother. He said, "You could be the Dean of Johns Hopkins Medical School and write concertos in your sleep, and she still would not approve of you." Sadly, that was true.

After a few years of therapy, there was enough trust to show my anger, and it erupted in full force. Now in reflecting back on the early stages of my therapy, I can remember when I became angry but sat on it. During one session I was talking about something and paused. Dr. S. interrupted, "Do yourself a favor and don't block." That made me angry. I remember thinking, "You SOB, you think it's easy to sit here and tell you everything, just unplug and let it gush—damn you." There were hints of an impending tsunami of anger.

I also talked to him about feeling needy and sucking affection from people when they were not aware of it. There was a "Star Trek" episode about an ugly monster that sucked salt out of men to keep herself a ravishing beauty. When I worked hard and received praise it sometimes filled the need. I could talk about that with some degree of comfort. But, generally I just felt better in Dr. S.'s presence. I would just walk into his office suite and immediately feel better. He didn't have to say anything. I felt I was sucking affection from him, but I couldn't talk about it at that time. It was too personal, and it was my secret.

The trip to Boston was just around the corner. About a week before I went to Boston, I started to feel just a little down. It was only a twinge, but it was there. I attributed it to the upcoming trip, extra experiments, and just working hard. But it was real. I thought about Boston and being alone, and somehow that frightened me. I wasn't worried about the presentation as much as walking around in Boston all alone. At work things were going well. I was rerunning experiments and double-checking the results that were to be presented in Boston. There were no major worries; our data was solid.

My few days in Boston were a Cinderella weekend. On the day of the presentation, I arrived early and was warmly greeted by Dr. K., my previous boss, and Dr. G. I listened to the main presentations and then when Dr. G. went up to speak, my heart started racing. It was my data that was being presented, and I wondered if it was going to be challenged. The first question came from the director of a competing lab. It was one of those typical academic questions that compliments the presenter, then offers a paragraph of their experience, and then asks a simple question, for instance: "Did you use the right buffer?" Several questions were asked in the same format. We passed inspection! I was thrilled.

We all went out to lunch and then spent time in the exhibitor's hall. I selected a new ELISA reader for our lab that could read each well directly, knocking off two hours of assay time. (The Dynatech ELISA Reader that I chose is immortalized in the movie "E.T.") I walked around in Boston, and I felt intelligent, accomplished, and appreciated. That evening I was invited to dinner at the hotel. When we sat down, Dr. G. proposed a toast to the research team. I told everyone that eleven years ago, I had celebrated my naval commission in Boston, and that this was equally a momentous occasion. My comment about being in the United States Navy was a conversation opener. It was a lovely evening. The next day I flew back to Chicago. On the flight home I told myself that this was the "new" me. Even if I hadn't made it into medical school, I could still accomplish a lot and be a meaningful member of the team.

I shared my Boston weekend with Dr. S., and he was pleased that things had gone so well. So was I, but it didn't last. And rather rapidly the elation went away, and the depressive feelings crept back in. I had some new work to do for the project. A set of basic immunological tests was needed to round out our research paper. I had to go to the library and read up on some of the old immunology papers since I was having difficulty with the protocol.

Instead, I found myself reading more about depression. Now this may seem counterintuitive, but reading about depression and suicide gave me a feeling of control. I couldn't fight the depressive feelings, but I had the control to do something about it if and when I wanted out. This worked well at work in the lab since I could be normal as hell in the research lab, but during assay incubations I could go to the library and read and be morose. I wasn't able to compartmentalize my day at home. At home I was a wife and the mother of a toddler. There was no escape hatch at home. I found myself becoming listless and easily irritated. Michael was not too sympathetic.

On Saturday, October 20, 1979, I took Anna shopping with me. As she lay peacefully sleeping, I took a notebook and made a list of the pros and cons of ending my life. The hospitalization effect was only temporary, Michael didn't understand what I was going through, and, although I never hit or hurt Anna, I could feel myself pulling away from her. Maybe I would be an abusive mother. Also, it was getting harder and harder to cope at work. It took too much energy to appear normal.

October 21, 1979. We were having an unseasonably warm weekend, and I took Anna out in the stroller. Michael asked where I was going, and I told him that I was really depressed and thought that walking might help. He was upset, "Didn't you work out your problems at Barclay? I thought you had a great time in Boston." I don't remember the rest of what he or I said, but I ended up pushing the stroller towards Michael and running away.

I had my keys and a few dollars in my jeans and went directly to my lab. I thought about what had happened. "Oh my God, I've finally abandoned Anna. I love her, and I have abandoned her. What is wrong with me? Why can't I keep it together? Why am I tormented with these depressive feelings when I work so hard to fight them? I don't deserve this."

I went to the nurses' residence and called Dr. S. from a payphone. I did not want him to know where I was, but I wanted to hear his voice. He called back and listened to me. Then he asked me if this could hold until the next session. I wanted to shout, "No! It can't." But instead, I acquiesced and said, "Sure." I went back to my lab and just walked around. Who else could I call? Could I call Michael? No, he'd be angry. Was there anybody else I could talk to? No. I felt trapped.

I picked up a vial of the barbital buffer salts and went to the nurse's residence cafeteria. I figured it would be easier to drink the salts if I mixed them in coffee rather than water. The cafeteria was almost empty. My fantasy was that I would down the barbital buffer, ditch my lab coat and identification badge, and start walking in some direction. I would not die on hospital grounds. I pictured myself walking on fallen leaves and then succumbing to the barbiturates.

I took the buffer salts out of my pocket and put them on my tray. I was interrupted by someone asking, "Do you mind if I sit here?" There were only a few people in the cafeteria with many tables completely empty. I thought it strange that someone would choose the spot opposite me, but I said, "No, of course not." He was wearing a lab coat, but I didn't know who he was. Then he made some comment that I must be on duty if I was here on such a beautiful day. I said, "Yeah, something like that." He was jovial and gregarious and continued, "Well, I just finished my eight (hours), and you know what, there's half a day left, and when you have half a day left, you've got exactly that, half a day left."

I've often reflected on the man that sat down across from me. He showed up at the time I was going to put the barbital salts in my coffee. Sometimes I just consider his choosing to sit opposite me was a coincidence; other times I like to think that he was an unnamed guardian angel.

I don't remember if he or I left the cafeteria first, but I got up and made another call from the same pay phone. I remember that I was hoping that Dr. S. would help talk me through this crisis instead of asking me to hold it for the next session. He called back, and I told him, "I don't want to live, but I also don't want to die. I am so sorry for my actions, but I don't know what to do."

Then came his cardinal act of mercy.

I will never forget his words, "Cynthia, I know where you are. You are at a pay phone in the nurses' residence. I want you to go to the ER. I think you need to be evaluated."

It was a clarion call, a directive, and I said I would go. I walked through the interconnecting halls in almost a trance. I didn't know what to expect at the other end.

When I got to the Emergency Room and walked up to the front desk, I was received with a cheery, "Hi, how can we help you?" It dawned on me that they saw the lab coat and thought I was a just another tech who needed to borrow something. (As techs we knew that the ER was the one storeroom that never closed in case you needed a bottle of saline or a syringe.) For one millisecond, the thought flashed through my mind to ask for a bottle of saline and just leave, but that thought was countered with, "And then what will you do? Anyway they're probably going to call Michael and send you home with a slug of Valium."

I told them, "I'm not here for work; I'm here for me." I told them I was having trouble with suicidal thoughts, and my doctor wanted me to be evaluated. Someone popped up and asked, "Are you actively suicidal now?" I told them "No, I came here." At which point someone else said, "Call psych back." I was told that the psych resident on duty, ROD, would be there shortly. While I was waiting for him, I made a promise to myself that I wouldn't minimize or aggrandize, that I would be completely honest. I would play it "*mf*" (mezzo forte, medium loud).

After the general questions, which included how long I had been in therapy with Dr. S., he asked how long I had been thinking about suicide. I told him about two weeks. At which point he said, "You didn't explore those feelings with your therapist?" The word "explore" just made me angry. I thought, but did not say, "You expect me to fillet myself and just tell you everything?" Then he asked me why not, and I said I didn't know. I did know, and therefore I had already broken the promise to myself.

They told me that I was being admitted to the Psychosomatic and Psychiatric Institute (P & P I). I remember asking, "Do you want me to walk over? I know where it is." They responded, "Oh, no, we'll take you over." A few minutes later two linebacker type security men showed up and escorted me to their car and drove me the two blocks to P & P I.

I was taken to Three North. The minute they unlocked the door, I knew that this ward was different. There were small single rooms on each side. They showed me to my room. It was very small; it only had a mattress on a pallet (not a standard bed), and the window was covered with heavy grating. There was nothing else in the room.

I thought to myself. "OK, you've bottomed out; it can't get much worse than this."

I called Michael and asked him to bring me some clothes and toiletries. When he came up to the third floor, I could see he was juggling holding Anna and holding the suitcase. I just felt awful seeing him struggle. I saw Anna briefly and was flooded with guilt feelings over what I had done. I signed a five-day release.

The overhead light in my room had two settings, dim and bright, therefore a patient could always be seen by staff. But my light was broken, and it only functioned on "bright." I was exhausted from the day's events and just wanted to sleep. I asked the staff if I could switch rooms, but they said no. I tried sleeping but couldn't. I lost my cool and told them with heated voice that even the Geneva Convention allowed prisoners to sleep.

The next morning Dr. B of the Michael Reese Health Plan (my insurance) saw me. He asked some of the same questions that the ROD had asked the day before. He also told me that I needed to rescind the five-day release. Since I was being taken care of by the MRHP, and he was in charge, in five days I would be transferred to the Illinois State Psychiatric Hospital if I didn't rescind the five-day release. Dr. S. came by that evening and told me that he was studying for his boards and could not treat me until he was finished. The next week I was kept on the unit, and a "rent-a-shrink" saw me daily.

During that first week I was rather frantic that I needed to leave the hospital. My birthday was on the following Sunday, October twenty-eighth. I knew that if my parents would call, they would find out that I was in the hospital, and in my mother's eyes I would be considered a loser for the second time. I pleaded with the staff to tell Dr. B. that I was stable enough to go home. When that didn't work, I started demanding them to let me go (obviously less effective). One nurse said, "What is your rush? You need to be here." I didn't believe her, and I thought she was being cruel.

Finally I was able to start working with Dr. S. The first time I saw him, he said, "Grab your sweater; we're going to take a walk." How did he know that I needed to walk?

The first issue we worked on was why I hadn't told him about fighting the suicidal feelings. I told him it was because he seemed pleased with my progress, and I didn't want to disappoint him; I didn't want to fail him. He told me emphatically, "You're neither my child nor my resident; you can't fail me." Intellectually I knew what he was saying. There was no timetable for me to get well, and he didn't hand out grades, but I was deeply hurt by the comment. In reflection, I wish I would have had the courage to say, "Will you run that by me again? The part about I can't fail you, because it just sliced right through me." (But I am here now, and I was there back then.) My four-year old psyche heard, "You can't fail me, because I don't care."

I stumbled around for a few days thinking that I was just a locked-up client, and he didn't give a damn. But every morning he came and we talked, and I started to think that maybe, just maybe, he did care. However, I still clung on to my suicidal thoughts as the ultimate weapon against the staff and him.

We continued to talk about my suicidal feelings, and surprisingly he never admonished me for having them. They were a symptom not a curse. I came up with the "high card" theory. I told him that being suicidal in a hospital environment was equivalent to holding the ace of spades. But, around here everybody was going to do their best to keep me from playing the card. And for me to get well, I would eventually have to discard the ace. As I thought about the high-card theory, I finally realized that I had to discard the ace. It wasn't a matter of "if," it was a matter of when. I asked one of my tech friends to buy a deck of cards. Sometime in November, I asked one of the nurses to put the ace of spades on my chart. I was making progress.

But progress wasn't going from point A to point B; it was hardly a linear route. My brother came and visited me. At first the visit was very supportive. He told me what he had gone through when my mother would send him out of the house, before she would start yelling and punishing me. He told me that he was so very angry with her, but worse, that he felt so helpless. He sometimes would go far from the house to avoid hearing her screaming, but that would make him feel guilty. And if he stayed within earshot of what was going on, he sometimes would get physically ill.

Sadly, I wasn't the only one that had suffered. At the end of his visit, he told me that he thought that Michael wasn't as supportive as he might be, and that I might be better without him. I knew that our marriage was very stressed with my emotional volatility, but I didn't think that it was falling apart. I thought about what he said and blamed myself for the appearance, at least to my brother, of a failing marriage.

And what did I do? I sat down and wrote out my "last will and testament." I folded the paper and put it in my pocket. But, I was quite manipulative in those days and ensnared one of the teen patients. I just happened to leave the paper on the table and the teen picked it up. He read it, panicked, and showed it to the nurse. (Pretty transparent, right?) Well, I was put back on suicide precautions and got a lot of attention.

After a week, Dr. S recommended that I start activities therapy. The staff felt that I was stable enough to leave the unit for a few hours each day, and the activity therapists were coming to interview me. After being cooped up on Three-North for two weeks, the thought of getting off the unit was exhilarating. I changed my clothes, combed my hair, sat up straight, and was as cheerful as I could be during the interview. I wanted to pass inspection. The activity therapists talked about what was available: arts and crafts, cooking classes, a place for coffee and chatting. They also asked me a few questions. Finally, they said they would let me know when I would be able to come down. As they left, I overheard Dave, one of the therapists, remark, "Boy, is she angry." I thought, "You are a real jerk. I am not angry. I am depressed."

Dr. S., M.D.

The next day I was escorted to the activities room. Much to my surprise and disappointment there was no piano. This time I would not be able to serenade the staff.

Dr. S. initiated couple's therapy with a social worker from Northwestern. Our first few sessions were at MRH. The first session was scheduled for November seventeenth. Twelve years before I had given my senior piano recital on that same day; now I was venturing into couple's therapy. Although I was very anxious about the meeting, the first session went well. The second session did not, and once again I had to move my marker back a couple of spaces.

Still, there was a thread of progress. I was talking to the nurses and relaxing a bit more. I wasn't trying to fight the system that everything, absolutely everything, was locked up. (I even had to ask the nurses for permission to use a pencil or my toothbrush.) Essentially, I was calming down and realizing that I was not just transiently depressed but that I was ill. I had a choice of thrashing around and being negative, or realizing, as one of the nurses had said, "The best way to get out of here is to concentrate on being here."

I had a change in perspective, and Dr. S. moved me to the healthiest of unhealthy units, Three East and West. The atmosphere was more like Barclay, and the patients weren't quite as disturbed. Being on that unit gave me the opportunity to go back to work while still living at the hospital. It afforded a gentle transition back to my normal life. Every morning the staff would give me my lab coat and keys, and I would head through the tunnels to Cummings where I worked. This was in the middle of December, and labs were just lightly percolating. There were a lot of holiday parties. Friends would ask me how I was, and my general response was, "I'm slowly getting there."

I spent Thanksgiving and Christmas of 1979 in P & P I. By Thanksgiving, I was experiencing longer stretches of being non-suicidal. Dr. S. stopped by briefly on Thanksgiving Day, and I remembering asking him, "Why do they keep feeding us? At group therapy they gave us sweet rolls and coffee, the morning activity was baking bread and then eating it, and for lunch we made pizza!" He said, "It's your basic O.G. day—oral gratification." I remember laughing.

On Christmas day, Michael, Anna and my in-laws visited me. I was truly happy to see everybody, especially Anna. After the visit, when I went back on the elevator, I wasn't flooded with guilt feelings that I had abandoned her, or that I had angered Michael by being hospitalized. I just knew it felt good to be around them. I thought, "I think I am ready to go home."

I was discharged early in January. I was glad to be home. The house was in utter disarray, but it didn't matter. I stayed a few days at home and then went back to work.

I have found that if you wear a lab coat, you can walk just about anywhere in a hospital, and no one will look askance. I found out that the FOIA would allow one to get a copy of their hospital chart. Wearing a lab coat made it that much easier. I was sort of obsessed about what the staff and Dr. S. had written about me.

As I read their entries, they had nailed my behavior accurately. At times, it was almost embarrassing. So many of the awkward things I did were just childishly asking for attention, like the evening I "ran away" but hid in the activities room. Ouch!

One thing I wasn't expecting was my diagnosis: depressive reaction in a borderline personality. At my next session, I asked Dr. S., "So, what does borderline mean?" He somewhat tossed it off by saying it was sort of a wastebasket classification. I told him, "You know, I know I am not psychotic. The Schaumberg police are not going to take over the world, but I always felt I was worse than simply neurotic. I've done some reading, and it resonates. The idea that you desperately seek love and attention, but when it is offered you do something to repel the person, and that you are then very sensitive to rejection and separation."

"According to what I have read, a lot of borderlines act out, have job instability, and sometimes are promiscuous or use drugs. That doesn't fit. Also, I don't find myself getting as angry as some of the patients profiled in the papers." (The anger and rage would come later.) "But, in some way it gives me hope, because it's a known entity."

In 1981, I flew down to Corpus Christi, Texas, in February between my parents' birthdays. I hadn't seen them, but more importantly they hadn't seen Anna since April 1979. Anna was now talking, and she was delightful. When I first arrived I received a warm embrace from both of them. They couldn't wait to hold Anna, and my mother had made a special play area for her.

My mother, who was newly diagnosed with Parkinson's, seemed to be doing OK. I thought all was well. I was wrong. Although I tried to avoid being with my mother alone, it eventually happened. She started with, "I have it all figured out, Cynthia. You're not depressed, you just had a delayed postpartum reaction." (Is there such an animal?) The second, longer hospitalization is because you have found that you are emotionally ill-equipped to be a mother." I remember thinking, "Oh, God, where is Dr. S., what can I say to this woman?" I said, "I think I am a good mother." She followed with, "Not if you abandon your child for almost three months." I was surprised that she hadn't counted the exact number of days.

I was speechless. I thought, "You're really something. I was in the hospital because I was suicidal, because I was trying very hard to do something that would gain your approval. Do you realize how much outpatient psychiatry costs in Chicago? And yet, I found the time and money to come down and visit you? I don't really want to be here, but I love you enough to come down with your only grandchild, my daughter."

My mother even had the gall to attack my therapists. In 1967, when I was seeing Dr. Hauer, a psychologist, she told me that psychology was passé and that psychiatry held the greatest promise for mental illness. Now I was working with Dr. S., a psychiatrist, and she changed her tune and said that psychiatry was nothing more than expensive drugs masking the real problems. When she attacked Dr. S., I reminded her that she had previously attacked Dr. Hauer. She was a bit flummoxed. I quickly replied, "You're right, psychology and psychiatry may take different approaches, but I am so screwed up I need both." Silence from the couch.

The fuse was lit, and American Airlines didn't help either. On the way back from Corpus Christi, we had to change planes in Dallas, one of the worst airports for changing planes. Because Anna was barely three years old and couldn't walk quickly, we were among the last to reach the gate to board the plane for Chicago. When we got to our assigned seats, a couple was sitting in them. We both held tickets for the same seats, but they were buckled up. The attendant told me that American would fly me out later and give me compensation. The compensation was $400, but I had to wait four hours for the next flight. Anna was tired and fussy. When I got off the plane, I sort of lost my cool and barked at the attendant, telling her that a mother and young daughter should get priority over a middle-aged couple.

The pot was boiling.

I started to get angry during sessions. Sometimes Dr. S. would say something that ordinarily wouldn't have triggered a defensive response from me, but now whether he was straightforward, calming, or instructive—I would become angry. At home, I wasn't in much better control. I threw a couple of mugs at the wall. But, I discovered there was a payoff for expressing anger.

Anger = Anti-depressant relief

After years of having the "hate vector" point inward, the vector had now turned around 180 degrees.

During sessions we talked about expressing anger and better modes of dealing with the anger. That did not satisfy me. I was angry, and I wanted him to know it. Did he know how very angry I was? I didn't think so, but I had to let him know. On the way out of his office, I took a glass ashtray and threw it at his door. My fantasy was that the glass door would shatter into bits of glass. Instead, the door withstood the impact, and the ashtray broke in half. I should have quickly left, but I didn't. Dr. S. walked outside his door, saw me, and told me that if I didn't leave immediately, he would be forced to call building security.

At the next session we talked about what I had tried to do: break his door. I told him it was the "borderline demons," and I just wanted to smash his door to smithereens. I remember he said, "If I thought it would help you, I'd arrange it." He suggested writing down my raging thoughts. I was way past the point of using pen and paper to exorcise my anger.

I never liked visiting Dr. S. at his office. Even if I would be on the bus or hospital shuttle and would tell myself to be forthright and sincere at the next session, the minute I would see his full name and M.D. on the door, it would trigger a less forthright, less sincere, competitive response. It was partly because he was an M.D., and it was also that I was angry for having to pay for help and affection, when it wasn't my fault that I didn't receive it in the first place. And so I had a plan that I thought was exceedingly clever.

Dr. S. might hate me, but he would never forget what I did.

I was going to take his name off the door. This took research, practice, and preparation. I first had to find out what type of paint was used for glass. Then I had to ask my friends in chemistry what solvent would remove that type of lacquer paint. They told me that trichloroethylene would do the job. TCE is a very strong and toxic organic solvent. They warned me about its strength, "Don't wear rubber gloves; TCE will eat right through them."

Then I had to practice using the solvent. I found that the solvent easily removed paint on glass, and the job could be done in minutes.

Now I had to case the floor at 180 North Michigan Avenue. The coming and going of professionals and clients was too erratic in the afternoon. I chose the morning, and, for one solid week, I charted the entrance and exit of the professionals on the fifth floor in the morning. Most of them had pretty regular schedules, like the guy that went to his office and then went downstairs to get some coffee. He was usually gone about fifteen minutes. After one week of "casing the joint," I figured that I had a fifteen-minute window of opportunity shortly before eight o'clock. The job would take no more than five minutes. I was ready. The first day I went to do the job, I chickened out. The second time, I did it.

I waited for the person to come in at seven forty-five and then put on cloth gloves and applied the TCE. I started with the letters "S. C." which were easily removed. Then the "MD" I paused there. That's the degree that's helping me. Nope, he's got to know how angry I really am. "LAST NAME," just a bunch of Scandinavians who settled in the Midwest. MIDDLE INITIAL, sorry, that goes too. Then I was down to his FIRST NAME. I thought of him as a kid, a high school student, an English major, a med student, a psychiatric resident—nope, sorry, that goes too.

The deed was done. I was just putting my rag away when I heard the elevator arrive. No one was supposed to be coming. The person walked right by me, right by the clean door, and noticed nothing. I put the TCE in my tote bag and took the elevator down. When the door opened, I saw the guy who was supposed to come at five after eight and told him that he was five minutes behind schedule.

Talk about exhilaration. Unfortunately, the invincible feeling didn't last that long. Worry set in shortly, and when I got to work, I panicked that I might get a call that Dr. S. had dropped me. Like a criminal returning to the scene of the crime, I went to the next session. He hadn't even noticed it; a patient had asked him if he was moving because his name was gone. (So much for trying to "destroy" your therapist.)

I really thought that taking his name off the door would be the ultimate cathartic release of the anger, and I would calm down. But it didn't, and unexpectedly I just became angrier. I was now dealing with rage. I have always found it interesting that the letters of the word "rage" are contained within the word "anger." It's as if anger is politely masking, "I'm mad as hell!" Things really got out of control when I cracked a window at P & P I with a pig, a lead cylinder used to transport radioactive substances. Dr. S asked me if I could control myself. I told him, sure, but I didn't want to control myself. I enjoyed the anti-depressant relief of acting on my anger. That was partially true, but I also knew the anger was escalating, and it was getting beyond my conscious control.

I spent almost a month in P & P I. When I was transferred to Three East and West, I saw some of the same nurses. I told them, that after years of being depressed, I was really angry and couldn't control it. One of the nurses said, "You'll be OK; you're just at a different stage of therapy." During that month, I broke a lot of ashtrays and threw a lot of stuff, but I would also come to grips with a painful chapter of my life.

During one of the first sessions, Dr. S. said he wanted me to go back on the antidepressant. Inwardly I thought, "Hell, no!" Outwardly, I just groaned. He then asked me if it would help if he prescribed Colace. I asked him what was that for, and he said that it was stool softener.

Never, ever had I been so enraged! I quickly stood up and looked around for something to throw. There was a phone and an ashtray. I envisioned myself throwing the phone at his head, knocking his head off his shoulders, with his brains splattered on the floor. Instead, I screamed, "You know too much about me!" I slammed the ashtray into the wall (it broke) and left the room (short session).

The next session I asked him to let me talk uninterrupted. I did not look at him nor did I want him to look at me. "You don't have any idea on how my mother's obsession with bowel movements has affected me. When we were in Japan (I was eight and my brother was four), my brother had some sort of fecal impaction. His treatment was multiple enemas that they administered at home. After they were through with him, my dad gave me an enema—just to be sure.

I cried and pleaded with them that I did not need it, but they did it anyway. After that my mother checked our b.m.'s daily. She would be furious if we flushed before she checked. Even when we got back to the states and I was eleven years old, she continued her ritual. If I told her I had a b.m. at school, she would make me describe it. She also liberally administered Castoria when our bowel movements "looked constipated."

If I was sitting reading or watching television instead of maybe outside roller-skating, she would say, "You're rather listless, you must be constipated," and out would come the Castoria. I learned how to lie, "It was brown, soft, and seven inches long" just to avoid taking the laxative.

If I spent the night at someone's house, the first thing she asked me was if I had a b.m. there. She was obsessed with the alimentary canal. She also would amend our diet, if she felt we were constipated. You can't have a cookie for dessert; the only thing you can have is some applesauce. There was what I call a "CF" (constipation factor) for every food we ate. If we would go to the buffet at the officers' club on Sunday, she would examine our plates and say something like, "You're eating too much cheese; you better take some more fruit."

When we moved to Texas, I was now twelve years old. She gave up checking our movements, but for her, everything had a fecal overtone. If I came home and she was cooking dinner, I would ask her what we were having. A common response would be, "Shit on a stick, and if I make it—you'll eat it." Besides calling me a G.D.S.O.B.G.F.N., I was also a "little shit." Of course, my room looked like shit, my music sounded like shit, and a lot of other things I did, had, or said would, make her want to take crap. (I know most of us sometimes express our frustrations using scatological language like, "Oh crap, I forgot something." But, my mother used that language so freely that I started to think of myself as fecal and tainted. I was sub-optimal, a *Brave New World* "delta."

I had a moderate case of acne and, of course, it would flare up before my period. She would say, sometimes at the dinner table, "I see you have a few pimples; is it because you are near your period, or are you constipated." This was in front of my father and brother. And the sad thing was, I was constipated, and I would try to clean myself out with laxatives and enemas. Then I wouldn't have to lie if she asked me. I used my hard earned babysitting money not for refreshments at the movies but on buying laxatives. My period would bring on the constipation, and so I started hating the fact that I was a woman. I would go to bed praying that I would wake up as a boy.

To this day, I cannot eat a meal without thinking about how the food will exit my body. Of all the things she did to me, slapping me, ridiculing me, embarrassing me, punishing me, this was the worst, because it invaded my body, and overall made me feel very fecal. Now, the fact that you know everything about me, from inside my head to my insides—well, it's too much to bear."

Thankfully, he didn't say anything, and I left the session room first. I got up and went back to my room. I tried desperately to hold back the tears, but it was useless. I was positive that he thought less of me and that he smirked to himself that I was never really a viable candidate for medical school.

But overriding those thoughts was the need to be held. I just wanted someone to hold me and say, "It's OK."

However, I was sane enough to know that physical contact was not part of a good therapeutic relationship. But I did think about the classic experiment where baby chimpanzees were presented with two artificial mothers. One was a wire mother with a bottle of milk attached. The other mother figure had no milk but instead was covered with a soft cloth. Most of the baby chimpanzees went to the cloth covered mother before they sought nourishment from the wire mother.

The next session Dr. S. shared something with me. He told me that usually when he saw his inpatients he checked their chart, saw them, wrote some notes, and moved on to the next patient. He told me that after yesterday's session he had to leave the floor to collect himself.

I thanked him for telling me that, because it nearly killed me to tell him what I did. It wasn't just about the icky subject matter; it was the idea that he had finally coaxed the hermit crab out of its shell. Only there are no more shells on the beach for the hermit crab. I told him that I felt like my mother had won. "There will be no secrets from me, dearie." I told him that I knew I read too much, but now I understood the borderline dilemma, "devour or be devoured." I told him that now he held the scepter and had the power to destroy me. I told him that I hoped he had taken the part of the Hippocratic Oath, "Do No Harm" with gravity, because I certainly felt extremely vulnerable.

I told him that I wasn't going to raise the suicide flag, but in all honesty I just wanted this to be finished. Game over. (I knew that as soon as I mentioned the "s" word, I would be transferred to a more secure unit, but I had to say that, because it was the God's honest truth. At that point, I didn't have the energy to lie or hide the truth.) As I was mopping up my tears, he offered a comforting, "We'll get through this." The fact that he said "we'll" instead of "you'll" was the verbal hug I needed. No matter what I had said, done, or thrown, I still had an ally.

One might think that after a few sessions like that, I would have become a little more mellow. However, there still was anger directed to my parents, especially to my mother. One of the nurses suggested that I write a letter to her. I said I would give it a try.

I wrote a letter entitled "The Unfulfilled Prophecy." I told my parents I took responsibility for my behavior, but a significant part of my problems today had been affected by the way I was treated as a child, teenager, and college student. I told them that the reason I was ill now was because I always thought the next stage of my life would bring peace between us. Now, there were no more stages that might fulfill the prophecy of us getting along.

I wrote how my friends said, "When you get in college and start making your own decisions, your mother will lighten up." That did not happen. When I was in therapy with Dr. Hauer, he talked about the rivalry between mother and daughter for a father's affections. He told me that when I was married, and had a mate of my own, things would be better. That did not happen. And then when I had a child, I thought that we would have something in common. That did not happen.

You told me that everything was inadequate: our apartment, Michael's job, my mothering. That's what led me to being very depressed: the cumulative knowledge that nothing I had done, had achieved, or would achieve could please you. In your eyes I was always sub-optimal.

I showed the letter to one of the nurses, and she said I should mail it. I believe I asked a tech friend of mine to mail it. I was afraid that the staff might trash the letter thinking it was just a therapeutic exercise. On the day that the letter should have arrived, I was quite anxious; however, I received no phone call. I thought that maybe they might have written back a response. Six days passed without a response. No one responded to my letter. I smashed several ashtrays and was moved to another unit.

I told Dr. S. that I wasn't really a patient, and that I was an undercover writer for Vanity Fair and wanted to check out all the units in P & P I, which I had managed to do in two hospitalizations.

P & P I ran out of ashtrays and discharged me on March 30, 1981, the day that Hinckley tried to assassinate President Reagan. Everybody was talking about the assassination attempt and that President Reagan had surgery. I thought, "Yeah, well I have just had surgery, and I didn't have the benefit of anesthesia."

I continued to work with Dr. S. as an outpatient, but it was hard because I still wanted to express my anger; the nuclear option was always within reach. I broke a bottle on the way back to my lab, and he initiated a "no damage" contract. If I broke or damaged anything, he would not continue to treat me.

In May I brought him a cupcake with two candles. I walked into the room and told him that it had been two years. "I am still here, and you are still my therapist. I think that's an amazing accomplishment for both of us."

There was still more work to do, and it would include two more hospitalizations. The fourth hospitalization was in July 1982. I wanted to have a second child but didn't want to conceive on medication. There were other stressors: We had recently bought a house in Oak Park, and Michael was working nights at Centel.

During that stay at Barclay I was broadsided with a new awareness after talking with one of the nurses. I told her that sometimes I thought that the only reason I was staying alive was because of Anna. She said, "You shouldn't say that." I responded, "No, I love her and it's only because of her that I am here." She followed with, "Don't do that to her. It's not her responsibility to keep you alive." She told me that I should stay alive <u>for</u> her, but not <u>because</u> of her and there was a clear difference. (I don't remember her first name, but I do remember a few details about Nurse R. She had twins and had parents who lived near Norfolk, Virginia.)

I have often wondered, if I had been told back in 1979 what I was told in 1982, would I have saved myself a lot of grief. Or perhaps, it was only then that I was ready to listen to what I needed to hear. ---"When the student is ready, the teacher appears."

The weekend I was admitted, a Californian attached forty weather balloons to a lawn chair, so he could gently float above the trees. Instead, he shot up 15,000 feet and an airline pilot was recorded as saying, "Either I need to retire or there is a man flying a lawn chair."

The last hospitalization was triggered by a visit from my parents in the fall of 1983. Everybody warned me not to invite my mom and dad, but I felt I was so much stronger, and I would be on my own turf. I planned for Mother's arrival and invited some of her old Chicago friends to a dinner party. Two days before their arrival my microwave oven blew a diode. (Even it didn't want to be around when she came.)

On the morning after the dinner party, she came downstairs to the kitchen. She was wearing a beaming smile. She told me that my eggplant parmigiana had induced a very good bowel movement. My hands were in the soapy dish water and on the counter was a large knife. I thought, "You will never know what those last two words have cost me. Maybe it's my turn to chase you around with a knife." My murderous thoughts were interrupted when my dad and Anna came downstairs, and he suggested that we go out to breakfast.

We were living in our own home. It was small, 1000 square feet, but it was ours. We had a garage and, although the second one was fourteen years old, we had two cars. We had wonderful neighbors. I was now commuting from Oak Park which was lot closer to MRH than Rogers Park. Michael had a good job which allowed for corporate advancement. I was making a fine salary at MRH, and Anna was enrolled in a top tier nursery school. How could she possibly find any fault with her daughter?

She dug deep and focused on Anna. She told me that having her start violin at age three was ridiculous. Anna clearly did not have a choice, and how we should never make her practice. (Hugs and stickers go a long way.) She continued onward. "Since you never achieved anything musically, you are trying to live vicariously through your daughter." (Anna was now playing in Suzuki book two.) She said that since both Michael and I were musicians, Anna would be raised in a neurotic environment. Then she took aim at me and pulled out a Freud card. "You are such a narcissist; you only think of your music!" (Hey mom, narcissism is better than sadism any day of the week.)

For Anna's sake I maintained my sanity through the holidays, but when January came I was in pretty sad shape. I also overreacted to the absence of Dr. S. when he was on vacation. When I was admitted I was both depressed and angry. One of the counselors on our floor pushed me a little too much, and I reacted by taking off my shoe and throwing it across the hall. The shoe accidentally hit a nurse and I spent the evening in full leather restraints.

Although we had talked about it during sessions, I dreaded the thought of separation and leaving Dr. S. I had become so very dependent on him. He had taught me to monitor my behavior better. I used to kid him and tell him that when things got stressful I would picture him as "Jiminy Cricket" on my shoulder. There were times, especially after the lengthy stint at P & P I, where I would call him just to hear his voice.

A typical phone conversation might go like this: "Pediatric research, may I help you?"

"This is Dr. S."

"Thank you for calling back. I'm OK, I just needed to hear your voice."

"Alright, I'll see you on Thursday."

"Thank you, good-bye."

Weekends were hard since he was not always on call. And so, to get through the weekend, I would play a game. I told myself, "Of course, it was his turn to cover his calls, but if I did call, the spell would be broken, and he wouldn't be available." Believe it or not, it worked about 90 percent of the time.

A letter I received telling me that he was changing to a hospital-based practice and shedding all his Chicago outpatients accelerated my separation issues. (I surmised that the hospital-based practice would be for adolescents. He was a genius with them. No matter how disturbed a teen might be, they would be like puppies around him.) The letter said that he would see his current roster of outpatients one more time—and then would make a referral.

I called his office and told them that I couldn't see him one more time and know that it would be the last time. I would rather have a coupon for one more session rather than never seeing him again. I made the receptionist repeat back what I had said. I told her that he would understand.

I was very fortunate to have had Dr. S. as a therapist. In my reading about borderline behavior, I had read that those patients were especially hard on their therapists. They were angry, clinging, demanding, and unpredictable. I fit all those adjectives plus when I am stressed I regress and become almost infantile. All I want to do is eat oatmeal and sleep with my head under the covers. There were many times he could have understandably dropped me.

Dr. S. didn't just adjust my camera lens; he outfitted me with a new camera. I learned how my behavior patterns are destructive. I learned that the fights with my mother many times led to reconciliation with hugs and promises to do better. So, from a woman who never demonstrably showed affection, I would have to fight her to receive it.

I also learned about the concept of "splitting." It is too repugnant for a child to think they are being punished when they are doing their best. It is less damaging to the ego to incorporate some of the "badness." Frequently, I became the bad actor so that the punishment that would follow would be justly earned. There were times I knew that what I did or said would make her angry.

Neither of those approaches works well in the real world. I have learned to be kinder to myself: I don't batter myself when I make mistakes or fail at some task. I also was released from the bondage of trying to do something that would please her. Sadly, that would never be.

I also learned that I could monitor my depressions. A depression doesn't have to go from feeling blue to being ready to jump off a bridge. I have the ability to stop the progression before I fall into a vortex, and I can get help before I become a danger to myself. I also learned that asking for help does not demean my character. He often said, "You don't have to be a hero." And I learned that acting out anger has only a temporary benefit. There are better ways to channel those aggressive emotions. (I still occasionally will throw a mug.)

He also gave me one more gift. When I am really stressed or fighting a depression, I can invoke his presence. During one hospitalization, he came very early (before six in the morning) to see me before he went away for the weekend. I was sound asleep. He stood by the door and lightly clicked his keys against the doorsill to wake me up. I eventually heard it, saw him, and got out of bed to walk to the session room. There are times, especially when I am reflecting negatively on the past, or just in need of comfort, that I think about him standing there and gently clicking the keys.

Dr. S. was a guardian angel, and it was I who won the lottery.

Kathy R. W.,
Research technician, Michael Reese Hospital Chicago, Illinois (1974-1986)

1974. Twenty-eight years old. I first met Kathy while I was working at MRH. She was working for housekeeping. She seemed to have more smarts than what was required to clean rooms. She told me that her young son had juvenile diabetes, and she wanted a job that she could instantly drop if he were to need immediate care.

I asked her about her education, and she told me she had a B.S. in biology. I told her that being a clinical technician was quite demanding because you had to keep up with the flow of patient samples; however, a research technician had a little more flexibility in planning the daily workload.

The seventies were the age of Pericles for medical research at MRH. There was always an investigator who needed a research technician. Research techs were not only well-employed, but we could also, for the most part, choose our job. I mentioned to Kathy there was a new doctor in hematology that was starting research. She applied for the job and was hired.

Although I received many cards from my pediatric technician friends, there were no technician visitors when I was in P & P I on Three North. Kathy was the exception. She would visit me frequently. She brought me fountain colas and milkshakes. She did my laundry, bought drugstore items, and brought me books to read. Since she always wore her lab coat, she could visit me at any time of the day.

I remember on one occasion I was in very low spirits, and I sort of barked at her that I didn't want to talk to anybody that day. She turned to leave, and then I asked her if she would just sit and stay with me. She did. For about fifteen minutes, she did nothing but sit on the floor with me. I have no idea what junk my mind was sorting through, but I knew that I felt better with a human being in the same room.

Kathy would invite me to her lab to have lunch, and we would talk. I was in weekly therapy with Dr. S. at the time. I would say, "Why is this taking so long? Why can't I get better faster? I am tired of waking up in the morning and while sitting on the edge of the bed thinking, "Well, do I go to work or kill myself?" She told me that throughout my youth I had not given up. She said, "I think there are probably many people who would have gone to drugs or alcohol, but you didn't. And because you held on, it's now harder for you to change." She said, "It's sort of like the movie *Ordinary People*. You are the brother that held on to the boat."

I also asked her if she knew I was headed for the second, longer hospitalization, which occurred in October 1979. She said, "Oh, yeah. One day you came down here for lunch, and half of your sandwich fell on my filthy, roach-traveled floor. You picked up the pieces of the sandwich, put it together, and ate it. I knew you were very preoccupied."

In previous years, I have found the holiday season very stressful. (Now, with my daughter and grandson I look forward to the season). One year Kathy stopped by my lab and brought me a small gift. I told her that she didn't really have to do it. "Look," she said, "it only cost fifty cents." It was a Christmas tree ornament, a small drum. Today, that ornament is put on the tree with affection and remembrance.

Kathy and I are still friends. She has a terrible back condition now that keeps her at home most of the time. I try to visit her when I can. I will always be very grateful for what she did for me— especially the visits when she would just sit on the floor with me. She was a guardian angel.

Kathy Jackson, R.N.

Psychiatric nurse, Michael Reese Hospital
Chicago, Illinois (1979-83)

1979. Thirty-three years old. I first met Kathy in December when I was promoted from the most secure unit at P & P I, Three North, to the most open unit, Three East–West. Kathy worked the night shift on Three East–West. I am one of those depressives whose sleep pattern is affected by depression. Although I can go to sleep easily, I may wake up early, around three or four o'clock in the morning. I would go out to the lounge and talk to Kathy, and I found that it was easy to talk to her freely. I was elated to be on a ward that wasn't so restricted, but I also knew that it meant I was closer to being discharged. I was worried about my coping mechanisms when I left. I remember her telling me just to think about tomorrow—not next week.

By this time I had become very dependent on Dr. S., and I wanted to know what she thought of him. After all, I had come to truly trust him. I would ask Kathy, "What's your opinion of Dr. S.?" She said she thought he was an excellent psychiatrist. But that wasn't good enough for me; I needed a stronger validation. I said, "That's boiler plate...am I in good hands?" And she said, "Yes, you're in good hands." I would also ask her what Dr. S. thought about me. And she would deflect the question with, "He's concerned about you." (In reflecting on those questions, what else could she have possibly said? But I was at the stage where everything required validation, and I was obsessed with what the staff thought about me.)

Soon after I came to Three East–West, arrangements were made so that I could stay in the hospital but work in my lab during the day. I told Kathy that I was thrilled to be back at work, and although I was worried that people would treat me a little differently, I found that no one treated me like, "The crazy one is back." I remember her telling me that I was ill, that I didn't choose to feel the way I did, and that I still had many strengths. Kathy was part confidant and part cheerleader.

As the holidays approached, the research labs were down to a skeleton crew. During the week between Christmas and New Year's, very few research technicians were working. One afternoon I found myself the only one on the fifth floor of Cummings where I worked. I walked around a bit and found that I was feeling suicidal, and I had returned to the feeling state I had been overwhelmed by in October. I felt that all the therapy I had slogged through wasn't helping me; I was back to square one. The lab was empty; no one was coming in the next day—a perfect opportunity to end my life.

I got out of there fast. I walked quickly through the tunnels back to P & P I. I couldn't wait to get back to the confines of my floor. I checked the activities calendar and quickly signed up for something. I felt that if I got busy with something—knitting, pottery, art, anything—I could neutralize the thought that was bombarding me, "Your mental progress is an illusion." I remember I tried to be as "adult" as I could about my thoughts. I told the activity therapist and the afternoon nurses. Telling them would not assuage what I was feeling, but I didn't want myself to be the only one that knew what I was feeling. I needed an ally.

Kathy was informed of my situation from the afternoon shift, and she called the ROD to see me. He wanted to move me to a more secure unit; however, it was late, and it was agreed I would move in the next morning after I saw Dr. S. Kathy told me that I would spend the night in the lounge.

The next morning as the docs started drifting in to see their patients, I kept my head down. I didn't want to see Dr. S., nor did I want him to see me. Anxiously I was facing the floor, and eventually I did see his shoes step into my vision. As I remember he was pretty gentle about my setback. I didn't feel he was angry with me; however, he agreed with the staff that

I should move to a different unit. I told him, in tears, that I really would miss talking to Kathy.

March 1981. For the anger episode I was put on Two North since there was no room on Three East–West. When I was transferred to Three East–West, I was delighted to see that Kathy was still working there. I told her that after many years of being depressed that I was angry as hell and came here to be exorcised of my anger.

I also told her that being angry had a great payoff—I wasn't suicidal. And, I was enjoying throwing and breaking things. She handed me a pad of paper and said, "Write down how angry you are." I told her I would think about it. She also told me that, in spite of my anger, she could sense that I was in a better place than I had been two years before.

The next night she was on duty, and I showed her a notebook that I had written in since meeting Dr. S. I asked her to read it. The notebook contained my thoughts about sessions, the information I would have surrendered if I hadn't "blocked," various analogies of our relationship, and a lot of writing about the torment of therapy, the pain of sessions, the feelings of dependency, and much about my suicidal thoughts. I also had lots of letters I had written to Dr. S. that I was quitting therapy, which I never mailed.

There were two analogies of my relationship with Dr. S. First, was a hermit crab. The shell in which it lives is the only protection for a hermit crab. As the crab matures, it is forced to leave one shell and find another, larger shell. The crab is exceedingly vulnerable to predators on the beach or in the air during the time when it is looking for a larger shell. In this analogy, I am the hermit crab, and Dr. S. is someone that is coaxing me to leave my shell, to grow, and to look for a better shell.

The second analogy was about a spider and a fly. Dr. S. was the wise but deadly spider, and I was the filthy fly who was snared by his web. The spider was huge in comparison to the fly. The spider told the fly that it was trying to reform the fly, to be a better fly. But the spider was also very powerful and could devour the fly at anytime for any reason. The spider lived on a remote part of the web and would check on the fly periodically. The trapped fly would welcome a visit by the spider even if he knew that he could be destroyed. The worst time for the fly would be when the spider would be dismissive of the fly and leave.

Kathy gave back the notebook in a few days and told me, "I'd hold onto this; you may eventually want to publish it." I asked her if I should show it to Dr. S. She said yes, and so I did. That was a major step forward in trust. He returned it a few days later but thankfully never commented on it.

Unfortunately, I was once again moved to a more secure unit and had to say good-bye to Kathy. She told me that after I got back home, I could call her at work any time. And I did. I still remember the telephone number, 791-3800. Sometimes when I would make my three o'clock in the morning calls, she couldn't talk to me. Other times she would stay on the phone with me for as long as I wanted to talk. Those were difficult days; I was still depressed, but I was dealing with "the new kid on the block"—my anger. Some of my calls were minor distress calls, and some were testing her with something I wanted to tell Dr. S.

I never called her unless I really needed to talk over "head" stuff, but there were times when the conversation was lighter. I talked to her about my daughter, Anna, who was three years old and had just started taking Suzuki violin lessons. I was told her that it was hard to listen to the scratchy sound and the poor intonation. I made some remark that, in therapy, I must be really "playing with poor intonation." She made some comment that I could look forward to a much better sound.

How many people, from any professional discipline, would say "You can call me anytime." Kathy helped me get through a difficult few years. She was a guardian angel.

Victoria-Grigas Hoffman
My mother's sister, Chicago and Villa Park, Illinois (1968-2005)

Fall 1968. Twenty-two years old. Before I joined the Navy and received my orders to Great Lakes, Illinois, I had only known my Aunt Vickie, my mother's older sister, from her brief visits or when our family would travel to Chicago to visit relatives in between duty stations.

After I reported for duty at Great Lakes, my boss told me that I could start my job in a few days, allowing me to settle in. My mother and I drove into Chicago to spend a few days with my aunt. The moment Vickie saw me, she just lit up, "My niece, the naval officer is here! I am so thrilled that you will be in the Chicago area; we'll finally get to know each other. Let's all go to lunch."

We took a taxi to an upscale restaurant, and when the waiter came to our table, she told him that I was her niece and a Navy ensign. My mother was rather silent during all of this. She somewhat smiled, but both of us knew that Vickie's spoken pride in me had outshined hers. We all ordered wine and were talking just casually when my mother said, "You know, Cynthia, with your personality problems, I thought that you might have washed out of OCS (Officer Candidate School)." It was meant to be a compliment, although it was a backhanded one. I thought to myself. "Oh no, even if I were to have graduated at the bottom of my class, I would have stuck it out. The thought of having to return to Sparta would have been a terrific incentive to finish."

Then my aunt said with big-sister authority, "Lillian, just be quiet, you know you raised a winner!" It was perfect. My mother couldn't say a negative word for the next two days, because it would have reflected on her, not me.

During my two years in the Navy, my Aunt Vickie and I had a lot of fun together. She was going through a nasty divorce and didn't have a lot of money, but we would still have a ball on the weekends. She would give me tips on how to shop at resale stores. "Always carry a magnet; if it sticks, the lamp isn't brass."

She had an apartment across the street from the Lincoln Park zoo. We would drink wine and munch potato chips while watching the traffic on Clark Street. On Sunday we would walk through Lincoln Park zoo and throw marshmallows at Sam, the polar bear. She was a cross between Sophia Loren and Auntie Mame. I didn't confide in her about my mother's mistreatment. I didn't need to do it at the time; I was having too much fun.

She was the manager of her husband's three-story apartment building which was heated by a coal furnace. During the winter we would have to shovel coal about every four hours and have to pull out the clinkers. Once she asked me to watch the water gauge. She told me not to let the water drop below the line. I asked her what would happen if it did. She said the furnace might blow up.

Vickie sort of lived on the edge. She could throw on second-hand clothes, put on jewelry and a scarf, and look terrific. She had a *joie de vivre* that was very infectious, and though her life, in terms of her residence and marriage was unstable, she never felt sorry for herself.

I asked her to help me pick out a dress for a cocktail party to meet the new ninth district admiral. We went to Marshall Field's, and as she was looking around, I also selected a few dresses. I tried on one dress, and when I walked out of the fitting room she exclaimed, "What, are you a Mennonite? Honey, you have a nice bust line, you need to show a little cleavage."

I introduced some of my Navy friends, including Lt. Serena Y. to Vickie, and she introduced me to some of her zany Chicago friends. I once went to an all night party in Hyde Park where the hostess served scrambled eggs at six o'clock in the morning.

Vickie and I would stay close through several milestones. I got married in 1972, and she remarried in 1975. She hosted my daughter's christening in 1978 and was also there for her confirmation, high school and college graduation. When I was living in Chicago, and she was living in Villa Park, there was a standing invitation to visit her.

I was going through some rough times when Anna was young and would usually make some excuse that I couldn't go. Her response was, "Just bring yourself, Anna, and don't forget your laundry. We'll figure out the rest." In 1983, after my maternal grandmother died, Bill and Vickie canceled their plane tickets and drove my grandfather's car from Florida to Chicago. Our family would have a second car, and I would be able to drive to work.

When I was admitted to P & P I in 1979, she wrote a card and told me their entire church was praying for me. She later delivered a package with a box of cookies and a red sweater. On the sweater was pinned a note, "When you feel bad, wear red." I remember reading the note and wondering what Michigan Avenue psychiatry would think about such advice. Actually, there was some merit in what she wrote. When one is depressed, any positive move is a thrust in the right direction. So, when I am depressed, I often reach for something red.

I did confide in Vickie and tell her what my mother had done to me. She said she was shocked but not surprised. She said that Lill, my mother, was terribly frustrated that she was smart enough to be accepted but could not afford college. She graduated from high school in 1939 during the depression and ended up being a bookkeeper. During the war, my dad, a naval aviator, proposed to her with a one-karat diamond ring and the chance to be a Navy wife, and she was thrilled. Sadly, her proclivity to manic depression (she once mailed me twenty nine pillow cases) was exacerbated by the stress of being a Navy wife—even though she outwardly took pride in being the wife of a naval aviator.

Vickie once said to me, "Cynthia, she saw in you what she didn't get." That surely doesn't absolve her of blame, but it offers some plausible reasons why she attacked me. Vickie also told me that when we lived in Texas (and the fighting with Mother was escalating), my mother asked my dad if she could see the base psychiatrist. He said no, because it might go on his record. There is a Navy adage that goes something like this: A good wife won't help you make Captain, but a bad wife might prevent you from making the promotion. I guess my mother realized that she had some problems, and that it wasn't "All Cynthia's fault all the time."

Vickie had a twenty-year marriage with Bill Hoffman. He died in 1995 on Christmas Eve. Our family was visiting relatives in New Ulm, Minnesota, when I got the call. I flew back to Chicago that evening. I helped Vickie take care of the funeral arrangements, and I later helped her move into a retirement home. When Vickie started suffering from Alzheimer's, I found her care. Although at the end she had no short-term memory, she always knew me.

On Monday, January 5, 2005, I was getting ready to teach piano after the winter break. The first three students called and canceled their lesson. I was a little perturbed; I felt that it was time to get back to a regular routine. I sat down and started to write a few thank you notes. I had written just a few notes when I put my pen down and started to look around the room. I remember thinking that I was glad that I had taken the time to decorate the house for the holidays (sometimes I didn't).

Then I was overtaken by a warmth and inner peace. For a brief moment I felt at peace with everyone and an untapped love for myself.

Then the phone rang. I was informed that Vickie had collapsed and had been taken to Elmhurst Hospital. We dropped everything and raced over there. When we went to the emergency room, we were quickly ushered to a private waiting room. I knew then that she had died. We waited for the pastor, did what we had to do at the hospital, then drove her caretaker back to the retirement home, and finally got home around midnight. The next morning I got up and looked at the stack of thank you notes. I then reviewed the events and thought about what had happened. I believe I had been touched by Vickie's spirit.

I would like to believe that there is life beyond the corporal body. If my aunt's spirit touched me, it was an incomparable gift. That token of metaphysical knowledge hasn't prevented recurrent depressions, but it has given me an inner strength to travel through them.

Vickie wasn't able to have children, but I was almost her daughter. She was like a mom to me for many years, a guardian angel.

Dr. E., M.D.

Psychiatrist, Skokie, Illinois
(1989-present)

1989. Forty-three years old. There had been a few changes in my life. After working thirteen years for Dr. G. in pediatric research at MRH, he invited me to move to Rush along with the entire department of pediatrics. During the first two years, I helped move the lab three times, and when we finally moved to our newly refurbished labs, they weren't quite sure what I would do.

Dr. G. was highly preoccupied with being the chair of pediatrics, and my immediate supervisor, Dr. B., decided that I would be farmed out to pediatrics at the University of Illinois to learn how to generate and culture monoclonal antibodies. In 1988, I said farewell to pediatrics and transferred to the department of immunology at Rush.

I was working part time at Rush (thirty-two hours per week) and teaching about fifteen piano students at the Suzuki Music School of Lincoln Park. My husband was working in the greater land of computers. My daughter, now eleven years old, was doing well in school and in other activities including studying violin.

Someone needed to pick up a sample from Michael Reese, and I, who new the terrain, volunteered to go. I picked up the sample and then went to the Cummings building where I previously had my lab. In 1989, Michael

Reese Hospital was just being used for clinical medicine; research was barely existent.

I went to my lab and found that my old key could open the door. I walked into my lab, and it was as if time had stopped. Nothing had been changed. Even my old sweater I used while working in the cold room was still on the hook. It was a very weird and unpleasant feeling. And with that *deja vu* feeling came the psychic feelings that I had while working in that lab during the time I had been seriously depressed.

I hadn't seen a therapist in a few years, and I felt I needed to talk to someone. The feelings I experienced were just too raw. I went to my Rush health plan doctor and asked for a psych referral. I saw a psychiatrist who turned out to be nothing more than a pill dispenser. She didn't ask me anything about my past or past treatment, even though I wrote it down on the intake sheet. She sat at a desk, and the drawer on her right had sheets with the list of medications and dosages. The drawer on the left had sheets with the side effects of the prescribed medications and the suggested remedies. When I objected to just being handed a prescription and reading material, she said that she herself was on psychotropic medication, and this was the best way to go. (No comment.)

I knew I needed to speak to someone, and I wrote to Dr. C., a local expert on the borderline syndrome. I explained that I had that diagnosis, had been working with therapist for about seven years, and was now looking for another therapist who was familiar with my specific problems. I received a scathing letter telling me that I did not have the credentials to label myself as "borderline" (even though it was written as a diagnosis on my chart). That could only be ascertained with several interviews by a qualified psychiatrist.

He did, however, give me the names of two psychiatrists, a male and a female. I wrote each name on paper, crumpled them, and put the papers in a jar. I selected Dr. E. When I saw that I had selected the female, I almost wanted to throw the papers back in the jar and settle for the best of five. But since fate had led me to Dr. S., maybe it was now time to talk to a woman.

The first time I saw her, we had a lengthy interview. As I was talking, she interjected, "You've done some good work," which was nice to hear. She seemed like someone I could talk to, but her office was in Skokie, and I lived in Oak Park. A few days later I received her $360 bill for the lengthy interview. I was angry. I sat down and typed an eleven-page letter to her listing everything that happened to me—childhood abuse, therapy, therapists, and hospitalizations—in the hope that it would minimize the fee for the time it would take for her to know about me.

I only saw her sporadically during the next few years, and I was off and on medication.

In 1994, my mother died. The events surrounding her death were almost comical. Anna and I had to stay an extra day in Texas after the memorial service due to a canceled flight, and when we got back home, we literally threw the contents of our suitcases on the floor, and packed up for the trip to upper New York State where Anna was going to be studying violin during the summer. Michael and I drove hard for a day and a half, dropped off her luggage, hugged her good-bye, and started on the trip back to Chicago. We drove back, almost without stopping, so Michael could be at work on Monday.

When I got back, there was a message to call my aunt. I found out that her husband, Bill, had fallen, broken his hip, and was awaiting surgery. On Monday I called my boss and told him that I would not be able to work for a second week since I was my aunt's closest living relative. I spent the next three days driving my aunt to the hospital since she had macular degeneration and couldn't drive. I stayed at Good Samaritan Hospital with Vickie and Bill.

By the time I got back to the lab, there were many serum samples that needed to be run in my three-day assay. Normally, I ran one assay per week, but since this was summer, and Anna was now at camp, I decided to run two assays that week to catch up, and I rescheduled all my piano students. The first assay went well. I was really tired when I started the second assay. I hadn't been sleeping well, and I hadn't been eating well, but I attributed it all to the traveling and extended mourning.

On the second day of the second assay, I went to the cafeteria, hurriedly ate breakfast, drank some coffee, and then collapsed near the cash register. As a hospital employee, I was taken to the emergency room and hooked up to an I.V. and a cardiac monitor. My boss stopped by and told me I should see my family physician before returning to work. "Any recommendations?" I asked.

I went to the physician he recommended and received a thorough exam with a lengthy interview. (I did not tell him anything about my head problems.) He told me I had a slight heart murmur and might have a mitral valve prolapse. He was called away from the exam room, and while he was gone I looked at what he was writing. It said "R/O MVP (rule out mitral valve prolapse), seriously depressed." I was really surprised at the "seriously depressed." I knew I wasn't eating or sleeping, but I attributed it to mourning, not depression, for this one reason: I was not suicidal.

There was not a single thought in my head that leaned toward self-destruction. And since I wasn't suicidal, I couldn't possibly be depressed. When the doctor came back he recommended that I get an echocardiogram and said that he was fairly sure I was depressed and prescribed an antidepressant. When I got home, I immediately made an appointment to see Dr. E.

That depression afforded me two graces: the first was, that although I was depressed, I didn't have to fight any suicidal impulses, and the second was my previous suicidal feelings had been real. There were times during the time I was treated by Dr. S. that I would ask myself the question, "Are you sure you're really this depressed, because this is getting to be repetitive and maybe you are conjuring up these feelings?" Many times, I would batter myself because I was experiencing suicidal impulses. I now knew that the intensity of my sadness and anger had led to a depression that caused moments of desperation and dangerous plans. What I had fought against had been real.

For the next thirteen years, I was relatively free of depression. There might have been times that I would experience a "lengthy low" and would see Dr. E., but upon returning to medication (I am not particularly compliant) and some counseling, I would return to the surface.

Significant events during this period were: hanging up my lab coat and my pipettes and going to full-time piano teaching in 1997; my daughter's graduation from college and her move to Baltimore for graduate school in 2000; starting to study German and attending a language institute in Munich in 2004; my aunt's death in 2005; and, in 2006, in celebration of my sixtieth birthday performing a full-length piano recital that included playing the first movement of the Mozart D minor concerto and three pieces I had composed.

I thought I would never be depressed again.

That would change in 2007. Blame it on the Clavinova. While adjudicating piano students for the Piano Guild, I met a teacher who had her students practice before their lesson on an electronic Clavinova piano equipped with headphones. I thought a Clavinova might be a good addition for my studio and purchased one.

I had to move some stuff to make room for the Clavinova and decided it was high time that I went through the boxes of paper that I collected from my aunt's apartment in 2005 after her death. I came across a shoebox labeled "letters from Lill."

The most recent stuff was on the top, and it was pretty sad. There was a birthday card my mother had sent to my aunt, and she could barely scratch out her name. If only I had tossed the contents before reading through the rest. There were quite a few letters my mother had written to my aunt during 1979–1980, the years that I was hospitalized twice for depression. My mother wasn't ill then, and her letters were typical of her correspondence: dense, several pages long, single-spaced, and typed on onion-skin paper.

I was not surprised to read that she, sitting in her house in Corpus Christi, Texas, had determined what was really wrong with me. She knew exactly why I was hospitalized for such a long time, and how my basic personality was at fault through a series of things that I had done when I was a child. Although it was hard reading what I had heard her say countless times, basically there was nothing new. According to her, I had an unstable personality complicated by the fact that I was highly melodramatic and a neurotic musician. What did surprise me was a letter she wrote during the three-month hospitalization in 1979–1980.

My mother suggested to my aunt that since this was my second hospitalization, I was probably going to be in and out of psychiatric hospitals for the rest of my life. Perhaps I should be committed to some state facility. In view of the fact that Michael did not have a very good job, he would be unable to take care of Anna. Furthermore, Michael's parents were several years older than they were, and therefore she and my father would move to Chicago to take care of Anna.

I showed the letter to Michael and said, "Can you believe this, my mother wanted to commit me?" I tried laughing it off, attributing it to the mental wanderings of a very sick woman, but the letter did its damage. The idea of her wanting to commit me wasn't as painful as the idea she wanted to get rid of me and separate me from Anna.

By the middle of June, I was seriously depressed. I saw Dr. E, and she put me back on an anti-depressant, but things didn't improve. She increased the dosage, but I had more or less retreated from the world. That summer I basically did two things: I taught piano, and I slept with my head under the covers.

From 1996 to 2009 I attended a weeklong summer piano institute in Kingston, Ontario. Attending the "More than Music" institute recharged my teaching batteries for the coming year. That summer I knew I should go, and that I would later regret it if I didn't go, but I had little energy or enthusiasm to attend. Michael encouraged me to go, telling me that it would be a break from teaching, and I could participate as much or as little as I wanted while in Kingston.

I told Dr. E. that I was going to go to Canada, but I was concerned that I might become really depressed. (At this point, the meds I was taking only allowed me to sleep.) I asked her if I could call her during the week, and she said I could her call every day. I did call her every afternoon. The content of what I said or how she responded wasn't as important as just hearing her voice. That was the "grounding" that I have in the past needed and found helpful. A kind voice is extremely soothing.

I did not have a terrific time that year. My teacher friends told me that I looked very tired. But, I did attend, and therefore my depression didn't cheat me from participating.

Aftermath: In August, I started a new combination of meds. Two weeks later I walked into Dr. E.'s office and said, "Is this how normal people really feel?" The depression had finally lifted.

2012. Sixty-three years old. In August of 2011, my daughter had a boy, and I instantly assumed a new role, grandmother. We flew to Baltimore to meet our grandson, Colin. We arrived the day before hurricane Irene hit Maryland, and we were without electricity for two days.

The weather was really only a nuisance. Michael and I were there to help in anyway we could. There was so much love surrounding little Colin. Andy, Anna's husband, went out to get ice, Anna went up to take a shower, and we were left to watch Colin. I burst out crying. I told Michael that there is so much love here, and that's not the way Anna's life had started. (My mother was bossing everybody around, and those first few days had been miserable. I remember looking at my lab coat hanging in my closet and just starting to bawl. I didn't think I wanted to be a mother.)

A year later, we flew to Baltimore to celebrate Colin's first birthday. Anna had planned a lovely party and had invited both friends and family. I spent a sleepless night comparing Colin's start to Anna's. I thought about how my mother had ruined Anna's first birthday, and how her behavior toward me that weekend was a "falling domino" on the way to my first hospitalization for depression.

When I got back to Chicago, the sleeplessness persisted, but I attributed it to jumping back into teaching with my thirty-eight piano students after Labor Day—and being a little run down.

As I lay awake in bed, I thought about my past, and I came to this epiphany: All the misery, abuse, bad times were going to die with me. I would do my damned best not to leave that legacy to Anna or Colin. I would not taint her with what happened to me.

It was three o'clock in the morning, and I jumped out of bed and went downstairs to my den. I asked myself if I really wanted Anna to look at this stuff. The answer was a resounding, "No!" I went to my bookcase, and I took all my depression junk— hospital charts, the countless articles about borderline syndrome, depression, suicide, separation and rejection, my journal of feelings written during therapy, and a lot of letters I never mailed to Dr. S.—and placed them in the garbage dumpster. When I got back inside, I congratulated myself on taking that positive step. I didn't feel exactly liberated, but I felt confident that I had done the right thing. All the "psycho junk" would go no further than me.

The next week I was getting ready to attend my annual church women's conference and was reading my mail and clearing off my desk. I had just received a letter from one of my piano parents with a $400 check to cover the extra instruction time I had given their son during the previous year. Her note said that it had been helpful and appreciated. What a morale boost!

I was stuffing my desk litter into drawers when I came across a copy of the letter I had written to Dr. E. in 1989 (which serves as the basis for this book). The contrast between the complimentary letter juxtaposed with the history of my life was just too difficult, and I felt angry at fate. Why, when I thought I had thrown everything out the week before, would I find that letter? What did I do to deserve finding that letter—now?

I took the letter with me to the church retreat, and the reptilian part of my brain had me read that letter over and over. I asked the retreat's speaker to pray for me, telling her that I had been emotionally abused as a child, and I just wanted "to let it go." She did pray for me, emphasizing that I was a survivor and could walk forward. I briefly felt encompassed by love; however, I went to the back of the auditorium and cried for quite a while. On Sunday, the final day of the retreat, I threw the letter in the kitchen garbage. I felt sure I would feel liberated by the time I got back home.

Just the opposite followed. I would go to bed and be swept away with all my negative memories. It was as if my memory circuits would not let me forget. And each night additional memories would come back, incidents that I thought I had forgotten. I lost about ten pounds, couldn't sleep more than two hours each night, and called Dr. E. for help.

I have emerged from this last depression. The sleepless nights helped me write the first draft of this book. Although Dr. E. told me that my "manic energy" generated the manuscript, she said that writing this book would lend a certain perspective to the events in my life.

Thank you, Dr. E. You have not only been a guardian angel but also a beacon for steadfast care.

Dr. Mike F, D. Mus.

Piano professor, College of DuPage
Glen Ellyn, Illinois (1996-present)

1996. Fifty years old. I first met Dr. F. at my church while he was organist and choir director. He frequently played solos during the service, and I admired his sound and technique. I was practicing the piano literature required for my Canadian piano institute, and I felt that I could use some coaching. He was helpful, and I liked his teaching style.

I was preparing to play a solo for one of my studio recitals and used our newly purchased video camera to record my piece. I was somewhat shocked and very disappointed in what I saw. I was expecting to see a confident pianist, moving easily over the keys. Instead, I saw someone whose fingers were locked to the keys and whose arms barely moved. (My piano playing was much like my old personality defenses, rigid and brittle.) I asked if I could study with Dr. F.

On our first lesson, he had me hold my hands above the keys and let them "free-fall-drop" to the keys. I couldn't immediately do it, because I was trying to control my arms, which is exactly the opposite of what he wanted. Finally, after many tries I was able to let my hands fall on the keys. I remember thinking to myself, "This lesson is very expensive; I hope there's more to it than this."

If Dr. S. rebuilt my personality, then Dr. F. rebuilt my piano technique. Fortunately, I didn't have to return to elementary levels of music. He still let me work on advanced literature, but he was patiently persistent and always working on helping me achieve a more relaxed, fluid technique.

After many months, my breakout piece was Brahms' Rhapsody in G minor. I finally was using the right technique, and I was producing a good sound. However, like any new ability, it took me several years to be able to easily incorporate my new way of playing. Many times I would fall back and use my old technique. Dr. F was extremely kind and patient.

I now have the three things that any pianist wants: tone, speed, and power, and I am playing pieces that I never thought I could master. This has not only given me greater confidence in my piano ability, but it has enhanced my self-esteem. I used to cower around colleagues who went to prestigious music schools, and I surely would never play for them. Now, I feel my tone and style of playing is musical, and I'll play in front of anybody.

I am still studying with Dr. F. Even after many years of lessons, I will lapse into old habits and have to be reminded of the technique. But more and more the technique is truly at my command. Most of the time I don't have to think about using the new technique; it's now the way I naturally play. I have also been able to incorporate this technique into my teaching. My students play beautifully.

Going from being a rigid pianist to one who now plays musically—was quite a trip. Dr. F was the guardian angel that took what I had and made it so much better.

Reverend Erik Gustafson

Minister-retired, Evangelical Church of Villa Park, Illinois (1979-1987)

1994. Forty-eight years old. I first met Reverend Gustafson when I started going to my Aunt Vickie's church in 1983. Anna had turned five, and I thought that it was time for her to learn about caring, sharing, and God.

By the early nineties, I had been through many hours of therapy to help me cope with what I had experienced during my growing years. With much professional help, I had come to terms with what my mother had done to me, and how those formidable experiences still played a major role in my current life.

But I had never considered forgiving her.

How could I possibly forgive someone who for the better part of twenty years screamed at me, embarrassed me, slapped me, threatened me, punished me severely, and told me repeatedly that I was just a G.D.S.O.B.G.F.N., that I was her cross to bear, and that she wished she never had me. How could I possibly forgive a woman who indirectly led me to believe that the only recourse I had to end my pain was to end my life? This was a step I never thought I could take.

Rev. Gustafson gave a sermon on forgiving. I don't remember the scripture or the analogies, but the take-home message was that forgiveness was as much for the forgiver as it was for the one being forgiven. It was a powerful sermon, and I knew that I wanted to take that step.

Throughout my mother's fourteen-year battle with Parkinson's disease, Anna and I would fly down to Corpus Christi a few times a year. In February of 1994, she had been hospitalized with pneumonia, was now bedridden, fed through a stomach pump, and mute. When I visited her, I knew her end was near.

But how could I forgive her? How could I, who was healthy and robust, walk back to her bedroom and say, "Mother, I forgive you for all the things you did to me" with integrity? I had to, in some way, make the forgiving mutual, not just an act of clemency.

By some grace I said, "Mother, will you forgive me for all the times I said horrible things to you?" I waited until she acknowledged my question with a blink signifying "Yes." "Because I want you to know that from the bottom of my heart I forgive you." I saw the tears run down her cheeks. By this time, I was also crying, and then as best as I could, I hugged and cradled her.

In June of 1994, I was running antibody assays for an in-vitro fertilization clinic at Grant Hospital. On June ninth, I checked the freezer; there were no patient sera. I called up my boss and told him that I was going to make a short trip to visit my mother since there were no samples, and Anna had finished school. (Our family had gone to Europe during spring vacation, and I hadn't seen my mother since her hospitalization in February.)

Anna and I flew down on Sunday, June eleventh. My mother was very weak. Anna and I stayed close to the house that trip. No trips to Padre Island or Aransas Pass. We stayed in the back bedroom as much as we could. Dad carried her out to the living room once so Anna and I could play some violin and piano duets for her. On Tuesday evening, I asked my dad to tell the story of how they met, their courtship, proposal, and wedding. (Their anniversary was the ninth of June.) There was some laughter and some tears.

Anna and I flew back to Chicago on the next day, Wednesday. On Thursday I was at work when I received the call that she had died early that morning. I, of course, broke into sobs. She certainly had suffered. But I was also crying for myself. By some unknown force I had seen her the day before she died, and more importantly, I had forgiven her. I would never have to say, "If only I had..."

I would never have to deal with that guilt.

Most of my guardian angels either protected me from my mother or came to my aid directly. Reverend Gustafson illuminated my path.

Conclusion

2012. Sixty-six years old. I have been in and out of therapy since 1965, roughly forty-seven years. I have been hospitalized five times—four times for depression and once for raw anger—and have had a zillion miles of outpatient therapy. What have I learned from years of therapy and life in general?

Patience. I am more patient with myself and others. Some of my Suzuki parents remark how patient I am, even if a kid isn't practicing. I am also more lenient with myself. I try not to set goals so high that I know I'll ultimately fail. If I become depressed, whether precipitated by something good or bad, I try to tell myself that I don't need to feel frantic, and that I will eventually reach the surface.

My past will always be with me. There is no "DELETE" key that I can use to "once and for all time" eliminate the memories of the emotional and verbal abuse I experienced. And sadly, each time I go through a depression, whether mild or serious, those memories are just not reminders of past events, but actually replicate the ordeal. I once read that the mind can not generate physical pain, and I believe that. I remember that I was in pain during labor, but I can't reproduce the painful contractions.

However, when I think about a painful episode, I experience the memory in high-definition reality.

I will need to cope with residual hurt and anger. Once, Dr. S. told me that he had thought of me after reading an article (nothing like flattery to perk up my attention). The article was about a man whose mother sat him on the commode at the age of six months and expected him to defecate like a trained puppy. As a result, he suffered terribly from chronic irritable bowel syndrome. Dr. S. followed with, "Cynthia, you will need to come to terms with what you experienced." That was a hard pill to swallow, and it had a sobering effect. Nevertheless, I was pretty positive at that time and thought that if I worked hard, I could come to terms with my past, file it under accomplished, and move on. What I didn't understand at that time was that I would continually need to "re-come" to terms with my mother's abuse.

Ironically, it is sometimes during blissful moments that I am faced with this challenge. Michael and I would always attend Anna's violin performances, and afterwards we always embraced her and told her, "You really were one of the best in the recital." It's times like these that I think of all of the recitals that my mother never attended.

The wounded feelings can pop up just that fast, and then I have to deal with them. Sometimes I look around the room, quickly do the math, and figure out how many other people might be walking in my shoes. Other times I tell myself, "Just enjoy this moment. You can allow yourself to be fully depressed tomorrow."

Sometimes I do what I term "shower rewrites" to change the ending of painful episodes. For example, when my mother threw the glass pitcher at me and I jumped in my car and drove to Dr. Hauer's house. Sometimes I end the scenario by not arriving safely at Dr. Hauer's house, but with an automobile crash in which I am seriously but not mortally wounded, and my mother finally apologizes and admits her mistreatment. Another rewrite is when I was in ninth grade and I cheated in algebra. Why would a good student cheat? Why the hell didn't someone send me to the guidance counselor? They might have found out that behind the photo-perfect military family was a rats' nest.

I am half my mother. Biologically, I received twenty-three of forty-six chromosomes from her. With that genetic inheritance came a predisposition to bipolar disorder and depression, but also some useful abilities. My mother was a bookkeeper, and I have always been good with numbers.

Conclusion

When I worked as a research technician, I could pull out the printed results and immediately tell if the experiment worked. I also have an affinity for learning a foreign language. My mother very quickly picked up conversational Japanese while we were stationed in Japan. I started learning German when I was fifty-six years old, and two years later I spent a summer in Munich at a language institute.

My mother viewed order and organization as the Holy Grail. She handled our moves like combat maneuvers. Rather than trust the packers, she did it herself to avoid breakage. She color coded and numbered packing cartons, and she made triplicate copies of the contents (outside the box, inside the box, and one for her purse). When we arrived at our next duty station nothing was broken, and what we immediately needed was immediately accessible. I am one of the sloppiest persons I know, but when order and organization are required, I am brilliant.

I am not unique. I look at it this way: 15 percent of the population is left-handed, 15 percent of the population has Rh-negative blood, and roughly 35 percent have lived through child abuse. That yields $(0.15)(0.15)(0.35) = 0.008$ or about 1 percent of the population who share those specific traits. Finite, but undeniably there are others like me. There are also many children who were abused far more severely than I was, and whose abuse led to permanent damage to their life and psyche. Thankfully, I am not in that category.

I am tenacious. I rarely give up. Of all my personality traits this is the one that is truly a double-edged sword. Growing up as a Navy brat afforded me wonderful travel experiences. It also forced me to deal with eight different schools including three different high schools, eight piano teachers, and from the time I was four years old, twelve different residences. I made it through college – albeit with the help of Dr. Hauer. I made it through the Naval Women's Officer School. I applied to medical school five times, and it took me four years to get my M.S. in biology via an evening program at the Illinois Institute of Technology. It took me ten years of summer institutes to complete the seven volume Suzuki piano pedagogy course, but I finished.

When I was working in pediatric research, I was asked to develop an immunological assay that would measure antibody to group B beta streptococcal antigen. To measure the antibody I needed to adhere a neutral antigen to a charged plate, which previously had never been done.

I tried every plate on the market and tried varying temperature, time, buffer, and matrix. And I had to keep tract of the permutations; that is I could vary only one factor at a time. Nothing worked. I then hit the library and spent countless hours looking for a way to attach the antigen. Finally, and almost serendipitously, I found an article that discussed binding a neutral polysaccharide to a protein via hydrogen cyanide.

I tried linking our precious polysaccharide antigen to a protein so that it would stick to the charged plate. I used bovine serum albumin for the linking protein because it was soluble, cheap, and available. It worked! The antigen finally stuck to the plate; however, when I added the positive and negative control sera, everybody came up positive. I attributed the disappointing results to my reagents or technique, i.e. there was a "bug" in the system, and I rebuilt the entire assay. Same results: all sera measured positive.

Finally, it dawned on me that the reason why all the sera measured positive was that I wasn't measuring streptococcal antibody. I was measuring antibody to the linking protein, bovine serum albumin, which is a component of cow's blood. Almost everyone has an antibody to bovine serum albumin by virtue of their drinking milk. I selected a different linking protein, human serum albumin, and finally had a test that could differentiate positive and negative sera. The above took two years.

Once I had a piano student who, to put it diplomatically, was awful. She challenged me at every step. Being a little discouraged, I asked the director of the school to listen to her lesson from the hallway. The director told me that I could drop her at anytime. Once my observations were validated, I pulled out all stops to teach her. After a few years of games and gimmicks, she finally started responding to me and became a fairly good pianist. She later was accepted at a prestigious residential high school, and she chose to recognize me as her designated mentor. I told her I was flattered but a little surprised. She said, "You never gave up on me."

That's the good side of being tenacious.

Perhaps the following might resonate with someone who has suffered parental abuse. I don't wish to anoint myself, but I was also tenacious in my efforts to please my mother or, at the very least, to avoid conflict. When I was in high school, I started my day at four o'clock in the morning to avoid going home, and I practiced the piano at school to avoid "jangling her nerves." During college I worked in a beer bottle factory in order to buy a car. (They handed out salt tablets to keep us from fainting on the line.) Although I had a great time in the Navy, after college graduation I needed to scratch being a teacher. I took pride in being a good research technician, a very accommodating wife, and a loving mother. However, in 1979 all of my cumulative efforts weren't able to sustain me, and my tenacity finally gave way. I fell, and I fell hard.

During therapy, my tenacity was a real barricade to progress. Even though I knew my life was falling apart, I wasn't willing to give up those behavior patterns that weren't working. My mother had been brutal in the intensity of her lectures. She would be mercilessly cutting me down, and I would be thinking to myself, "You can't get to me. You can't get to me. I will show you no emotion."

Unfortunately, those grooves ran deep, and I steeled myself to what I heard during a session and was reluctant to change. During the first two years of therapy with Dr. S., I was determined I never would cry in front of him. It was only during the anger period, when I was finally worn down and worn out enough, that I could show the hurt.

Michael once remarked that he thought I viewed therapy with Dr. S. as some sort of game. I was angry with his comment, but on some level he was right. My psyche initially viewed therapy with Dr. S. as a battle of the wits, and I was determined that I would win. Yes, I missed the boat. This therapy was quite different than working with Dr. Hauer while I was in college. In those days I needed emotional support and guidance since I was dealing with a mentally ill mother. Dr. Hauer was trying to prevent further damage. Dr. S. was trying to fix the wreckage. This was far more threatening.

Many times after a session, I would go home and write a letter to Dr. S. that I was quitting therapy. Behind the guise of wanting to end therapy because I thought it was expensive and useless, was the unconscious awareness that my tenacity was crumbling and worse yet, I was becoming dependent on him. At times I was a child begging for his love and attention and would never, ever miss an appointment. Other times I just wanted to shove him through a plate glass window for his trying to get to me. I was a hard nut to crack.

I am sensitive to rejection and separation. Because I was, in part, rejected by my mother, I am very wary of rejection from others, and I can also misinterpret change as rejection. When a piano student tells me they are not continuing, the first thing I ask myself is, "What did I do wrong?" The reason could be simply that the child would rather spend their limited extra curricular time doing something else, but I inevitably will assign self blame. This can lead to the depressive tumble. I didn't teach this child well......I am not a good teacher......I am a lousy person.

When Dr. S chose to go to a hospital based practice, I was devastated. After I received his letter, I pored though all my hospitalization charts and re-read everything he had ever written about me. I wanted, in some way, to hold on to him.

Some of my friends have often asked me, "If you are so sensitive to separation, how did you survive military life?" The answer is easy--hope trumps separation. Moving to a new duty station was a chance for a fresh start. At the next duty station I would be a wonderful sister, a straight-A student, and I would be the perfect daughter. I would be helpful to my mother, and she and I would get along. A new set of orders brought hope that things might change for the better.

I have often thought about this phenomenon with respect to the increased awareness of the difficulties that many military families face. Due to the stress of long deployments, combat duty, or the overriding fear that their spouse might come home in a box, their lives start falling apart. Then they receive a new set of orders which brings not only a change in location but a sense of optimism. Unfortunately, many times when they arrive at their next duty station, they unpack their old problems.

I can monitor my depressions. When I become depressed I sometimes experience perceptual changes. I don't hallucinate nor am I delusional, but certain things happen that let me know that I am starting to submerge.

I start to read things backwards. This usually happens when I am driving. It's not that I can't read in the normal direction, but I find myself reading from right to left. For example, speed limit becomes "timil deeps." At this stage the depression is reversible.

I may experience a lack of depth perception. Everything looks like a postcard. My memory, of course, tells me that things are three dimensional, but they appear flat. This can happen when I am walking down a hallway and no person is in sight. However, as soon as I see a person, my vision is "grounded" and my depth perception returns. At this point I am treading water. I can't easily move forward, but I am not sinking.

Sometimes I dissociate or partially leave my body. It's not like a near death experience when someone is circling above their clinically dead body. It's just that I feel I am watching myself doing something rather than actually doing it. I am driving and looking at my hands and think, "Just whose hands are on the steering wheel?" I also start to think, "What is going on? Am I vibrating at a different frequency?" Or I ponder the reality of the experience. "Perhaps this is virtual reality and I am not fully plugged in." It has its metaphysical overtones. At this point I am underwater and I can't do it by myself. I need what I call "CCT," conversation and cocktails (meds) therapy.

Family dynamics played a role. A psychotherapist, a former college dorm mate, reviewed this manuscript. She told me that if she had treated me when I was younger, she would have hauled in the whole family. She said that I may have been the identified patient, but in essence I bore the brunt of a dysfunctional family. I had never thought about it in those terms. By the time I got to college I knew my mother was nuts, but I always viewed myself as the weak link. I was the one that eventually sprang a leak. After all, my brother and father never ended up in a therapist's office.

Anger was part of the healing process. She also told me that my epoch of rage was actually a flight into health. The anger did neutralize the suicidal impulses, but I also felt that my anger was the real, wicked, and ugly side of me that had been unmasked. I draped a towel over the bathroom mirror because I thought that even my appearance had changed. My flight into health was not a smooth ride; there was a great deal of turbulence. I did a lot of damage with little remorse. Dr. S. was charitable and did not charge me for repainting his name on his office door, but Michael Reese's accounting department wasn't as generous. They garnished my salary for a couple of months to cover the three hundred dollars needed to replace the broken window.

Now I find it interesting that feeling irritable rather than blue is a signal that I might be facing a depression. If I am listening to a student play and think, "Just when the hell are you going to start practicing your scales?" Then I have to sit back and realize something is going on with me, not my student. But, I also have to resist the temptation to batter myself because I became angry. (Old habits don't die; they just get moldy.) It is better for me to put on a jacket, take a walk, and tell myself that I am doing OK, and that I am still in a lot better shape than my student's F major scale.

I have a sense of humor. I don't profess to be a stand-up comic, but I can find something humorous even in dark situations.

My dad had a terrific sense of humor, and he could nip my mother in the bud, especially when she was on some sort of binge. While living on the base in Argentia, she started reading everything by Freud. One evening at the dinner table she said, "Kaz, do you know you have an anal-retentive personality?" With out dropping a beat, my dad responded, "Sounds like a shitty outlook on life." Well, Freud didn't even make it to the main course. We all laughed and that was the end of her analysis for the evening.

One time my dad, brother, and I went downtown to do some Christmas shopping. While we were in the car, my dad asked, "Well, what shall we get mother? I responded, "A muzzle." Then my brother added, "And a leash." We all laughed hysterically which defused the situation, and we bought her a nice gift.

During the time I served in the Navy, Lt. McCain (Senator McCain) was a jet pilot who was shot down over North Vietnam and became a prisoner of war. This quickly made the news since Lt. McCain's father, Admiral McCain, was commander of all naval forces in the Pacific. At dinner one evening we were casually discussing what would break us down if we were imprisoned. One officer said that he could withstand hunger but not exposure to intense heat or cold. Another officer said that if he were subjected to loud noises or not be able to sleep, he might crack. Then they asked me, "Well Lieutenant, how long could you hold out?" I responded, "If they touched one hair on my head, I would tell them my name, rank, serial number, and.... the position of every ship in the seventh fleet." Even the senior officers at the table laughed.

I love one-liners like, "A Smith and Wesson beats of full house." or the first line of the play "The Lion in Winter," "Well, shall we hang the holly or each other?" and a favorite of mine is Woody Allen's, "Seventy-five percent of living is showing up." My favorite joke about suicide is: "Doctor, I am feeling somewhat suicidal, what should I do?" The doctor responds, "Pay in advance."

When I was in P & P I on Three North, I had this Wizard of Id comic strip taped on my wall:

First frame: The King says, "I am feeling blue, please send for the psychiatrist."

Second frame: The servant says, "The psychiatrist doesn't make house calls."

Third frame: The King says, "Tell him the executioner does."

Sometimes I will crack a joke during a therapy session. I casually told Michael that I had cut down on one of the meds Dr. E prescribed, because I felt like a zombie in the morning. He asked me if I had discussed it with Dr. E, and I told him no, that I would be seeing her the next week. Well, he was pretty upset, and told me that maybe I would get better faster if I just followed the doctor's orders. The next week I relayed our conversation to Dr. E. "Michael thinks I should do whatever you tell me. It's like if you told me to put a french fry in my ear, I should quickly respond with, "Which ear?"

Once when I was working with Dr. S, he asked me how angry I was. I told him that before this volcanic anger erupted that I could easily shrug off being irritated or angry. I told him that if he were to put a hundred dollar bill on the floor and say, "It's yours, but you have to cool it." I would say, "Bye, I'm going shopping." "Now," I told him, "There is no amount of money that will keep me from exploding." He chuckled and said that maybe I had invented a useful diagnostic tool.

Dr. S. enrolled me in a clinical research study at Northwestern University. The investigators were looking for biomarkers for affective disorders. At my next session Dr. S. asked,

"So, how did it go?"

"Fine, the interviewer took his time, but I knew he was a Ph.D. the minute I saw him."

"How so?"

"Let's see, instead of wearing dress slacks, he was wearing black chinos and his shoes did not go with his pants. I did not have the heart to look at his socks. His shirt was nice, but he was wearing a tie that either a student gave him or he got from Salvation Army. He had on one of those typical academic corduroy jackets with the leather elbow patches, but I think he has been wearing it since graduate school. Classic Ph.D."

"So, how do I dress?"

"Hopelessly M.D."

Most of the consequences of my mother's binges were hardly laughable, but this one was not only funny but one for the Guinness book of records. Just how many carrots can one eat?

While we were in Iwakuni, Japan, we were told not to eat locally grown produce. The Japanese farmers fertilized their crops with human manure, and there was a high risk of picking up the tapeworm parasite. There were posters plastered all over the base warning us not to eat anything raw off base. On those posters would be a picture of a life size tape worm that had been surgically removed from someone harboring the parasite. Those pictures were pretty repulsive.

My mother, however, was determined to eat fresh vegetables. She found out that soaking the vegetables in dilute bleach would kill all parasites. This first time she served us the bleach treated cabbage it tasted like coleslaw with Clorox. The three of us agreed that we could live without lettuce for a few years. When we got back to the states, my dad was looking forward to a few years of less strenuous shore duty, my brother and I were looking forward to real milk and television, and my mother was looking forward to enjoying fresh vegetables.

However, she went on a vegetable eating binge. One morning she woke up yellow. My dad took her to the naval dispensary in Coronado, and they quickly referred her to the naval hospital in San Diego. When she told the doctor that she had eaten about a dozen carrots the day before, that cinched the diagnosis: she had carotenemia, a type of vitamin A toxicity. Although the condition wasn't life threatening, it was imperative that she stay out of the sunlight to protect her vision. Like a potted plant or a vampire she needed to stay in the dark during the day. It took more than a week for the vitamin A to work its way out of her system.

My mother fully recovered. However, in her inimitable way of never losing face, she said that even though she couldn't eat yellow vegetables for a while, she could still eat green vegetables. My dad interjected, "Lillian, if you wake up green, you can just paint yourself white." When she was ill, we were all very concerned that she might lose her vision and were very kind to her. Now, I still get a healthy laugh thinking about the Bugs Bunny episode.

I was given the gift of music. I was never a musical prodigy. In my twenty-five years of teaching piano, I have encountered students who have a better ear, better sense of rhythm, better technique, and are better performers than myself. I do have a certain passion for music. Music has given me inspiration, comfort, identity, companionship, and recognition. During adolescence I listened to the sound track of *West Side Story* until the record wore out. I danced with "I Feel Pretty," and I cried during "Somewhere." I could also give the piano hell when I was angry. My mother thought I

Conclusion

was super neurotic, but piano served as a needed emotional outlet. During college, playing the piano and the French horn was many times my only sense of stability and identity.

In reflection, that may have been why my mother sometimes forbade me to practice. While sitting at the piano, I felt very feminine and quite lovely. My music served as a firewall between her and me—and she knew that.

Now, teaching piano has offered me an extremely rewarding career that doesn't require me to stop at retirement age. Music also provides a wonderful bond with my husband and daughter, and I enjoy being an amateur composer and creating my own music. The fact that I love and was able to pursue music was a gift that not only provided coping skills but has enriched my life.

My life is fairly normal. I enjoy traveling, watching foreign films, going to the opera, reading Michael Connelly novels, listening to my favorite band, "Chicago," eating anything with eggplant, and of course, being with my grandson. My husband, however, has to live with a mate who is always a nickel away from depression. His expression is, "I can tell your mood by the way you put the key in the door."

I have a lovely daughter and we have a warm relationship. I am thankful that she inherited Michael's mixture of neurotransmitters. She is stable, sensible, serene, and a wonderful mother. Not having a good role model, I made my mistakes in parenting, but Anna was always quite forgiving. She is also devoutly Christian. I once lamented to her that I was sorry she did not have a sibling. She said, "That's alright mom. I did pray that I would have a baby sister or baby brother, but I also prayed that you would get well. God answered one of my prayers." That is Anna. She has a great relationship with her dad, and unlike my mother, I revel in their ability to communicate on the same frequency.

I am grateful to be where I am. I am happily self-employed as a Suzuki piano teacher. My personal teaching motto is, "Teach the child, teach music, then teach piano." One of my jobs as a Suzuki teacher is to enhance the bond between parent and child. Sometimes during a lesson, I will pause and ask the student to give a hug or a "hi-five" to their parent to celebrate their progress. Admittedly, that might cause me to choke a little, but I still take satisfaction in helping to nurture that bond.

I am active in my professional groups, and I share the keyboard ministry at my church. I also have some wonderful friends. When I was younger I always considered myself damaged goods. Now, I know that I have been patched over quite nicely. I do bear some scars, but I know that I've won the war.

In 2000, I climbed my first mountain, Mt. Bleckwand, near Salzburg, Austria. It wasn't easy; I huffed and puffed all the way. Our Austrian friends, the Horvath family, gave me tips on how to keep going even if I sometimes needed to go sideways, and Michael was always right behind me. Reaching the top allowed me to see the magnificent view of the Salzkammergut. As I was looking at the indescribably beautiful view of the lakes and hills, I had a five-second flashback of a few negative events in my life. The knife, lectures, walks, the juice pitcher, the barbital salts, Three North, broken window, confessions.

Then I smiled and allowed myself to bask in the beauty of the moment. *Sehr, sehr schoen.* (So very beautiful.)

Coda

Sometimes I feel my life is like a play. I am an actor who was handed a pretty lousy script, and I wasn't able to delete scenes or edit the dialogue. I had a misguided mother who was always on stage, whether she was delivering her lines directly or behind the curtain. Even now, eighteen years after her death, there is the offstage Greek chorus waiting to chant her refrain, "You're a G.D.S.O.B.G.F.N., I knew you'd fail, I wish I'd never had you."

However, as the play continues there are people who crossed my path who protected me from her, sometimes protected me from myself, guided me, and took the time to teach me that the whole play didn't have to be a tragedy. There were people whose kindness, professional dedication, and love offered me some colorful scene changes, wonderful experiences, and infused me with an inner strength that will enable me to be standing on stage at the end of the play. A lousy script, yes—a bad life, no.

I have certainly asked myself the question, "Why was I abused?" I was a good kid, an excellent student, and certainly didn't deserve what I experienced. The answer is my mother was ill, she obviously needed treatment that she never received, and she foisted her emotional limitations on me. But it really doesn't help to mull over the question, "Why?" unless perhaps one is doing research. I also don't believe in pre-destiny. Never have. Never will. And I dislike the phrase, "God only gives you what you can handle." When I was thirty-two years old, I started unraveling, wasn't handling things well at all, and needed medical and psychological intervention. Because I was unable to help myself, does that mean that God loves me less?

No, if there is a thread of sanity or even of hope on planet Earth, it's the people that help each other along the way. May you not only have your cadre of guardian angels, may you also be a guardian angel to others. I was fortunate. I had at least seventeen.

Encore

And now, this is my final opportunity to thank all of those people, who throughout my life have been there when I needed them most, my guardian angels.

Sue, Dorothy, Jopi, Judith, Stephen, Gerald, Herbert, Rowena, Diane, Serena, Dr. S., Kathy, Kathleen, Vickie, Dr. E, Mike, Rev. Erik

How can I thank you for protecting me? How can I thank you for helping me when I was most fragile? How can I thank you for intervening on my behalf? How can I thank you for making me do the right thing? How can I thank you for making me laugh? How can I thank you for the dogged perseverance that it took to change my perspective and behavior? How can I thank you for being a true friend? How can I thank you for helping me grow? How can I thank you for giving me the strength to forgive? How can I thank you for just being there?

Words falter.

Bravo! Brava!

If it takes a village to raise a child, then it took everyone I knew to write this book. Thank you Carol Olmstead for your comment, "There are many books on child abuse; try a different approach." Dr. Karen Beatty for your long and empathic telephone call and your suggestions to include my father's role and the effect of being a military dependent, Beth Franken for foraging through the first grammar-mangled draft and writing the summary, Pastor Ken Johnson and Dr. Susan Scherer for your moral support and endorsements, Kathy Wos for your unexpected and generous financial gift, Martha Brunelle for reading the entire manuscript although it was a Herculean task, Ronald Balson for introducing me to online publishing, and Reverend Don Lindman for guiding me to CreateSpace.

I would also like to thank Mydella Papierniak, my mother-in-law, for always being there for Anna, even when I wasn't physically or emotionally available; Rudolf Strahl, whose sincere and encouraging teaching style has inspired me both personally and professionally (*Vielen dank*), Dr. Mary Kelly, our family physician, who patiently understands that physical ailments often follow mental crashes, and Nina Drath, concert pianist, for being a colleague and a mentor. Her advice, "Just forget the rest and seek beauty." is well worth keeping.

I would like to acknowledge the More than Music institute of Kingston, Ontario, whose unique, non-competitive philosophy provided a self-affirming atmosphere. Thank you Valery Lloyd-Watts, Clayton Scott and the late Carole Bigler. I'd like to thank the covenant women of the Evangelical Covenant Church of Villa Park, Illinois, for their friendship and circle of love, which continually offers healing and restoration. There is so much more to Bible study than reading scripture.

A standing ovation goes to the CreateSpace.com team. Thank you for your professionalism and sensitivity. Thank you Laura Burns, editor, for your positive and supportive comments which galvanized my spirit and strength to continue this project.

For my brother Charles. You also were a part of our "dysfunctional family dance." You had a difficult role: keep dancing but look the other way. I realize it took an emotional toll on you, too. Nevertheless, I still have many good family memories, especially when we traveled or were all in the water.

Thank you Michael for all your support and love and for your patience during hospitalizations and setbacks. I know it isn't easy living with someone that occasionally wears the same clothes for a week or starts organizing and cleaning at four o'clock in the morning. Thank you for being understanding when I said I needed to write this book. And, you are the greatest dad that Anna could ever have.

My dear Anna. I wrote this book not to elicit pity or sympathy but to set the record straight. The most important result is, that because of my seventeen angels, the abuse did stop with me. I only have to look at you to know that. You are a beautiful person, a loving wife, and a radiant mother. I couldn't think of a better gift I could receive.

Cynthia Papierniak, Michael Papierniak,
Colin Durbin, Anna Durbin, Andrew Durbin

Baltimore, Maryland (2012)
Photo by Dennis Drenner
Permission granted

Cynthia (Kanapicki) Papierniak was born in 1946 during the first wave of "bumper crop" babies after WWII. Her Navy family moved thirteen times before she attended college. She earned her B.A. in Music Education from Montclair State College, New Jersey, studying piano and French horn. In 1968, she was commissioned as an officer and served in the US Navy for two years. She received her M.S. in Biology from the Illinois Institute of Technology and worked as a medical research technician at Michael Reese, Rush, and Grant hospitals.

Currently she teaches piano and composes music. Her husband, Michael, plays the French horn, and her daughter, Anna, a violinist, lives in Baltimore with her husband, Andrew, and their son, Colin. Cynthia resides in Oak Park with her husband, two dogs, and two pianos.

Comments on Seventeen Guardian Angels are welcome.

seventeen.angels@yahoo.com

Made in the USA
Charleston, SC
26 November 2013